Cambridge Elements ≡

Elements in Religion and Violence
edited by
James R. Lewis
University of Tromsø
Margo Kitts
Hawai'i Pacific University

SACRED REVENGE
IN OCEANIA

Pamela J. Stewart
University of Pittsburgh

Andrew Strathern
University of Pittsburgh

CAMBRIDGE
UNIVERSITY PRESS

CAMBRIDGE
UNIVERSITY PRESS

University Printing House, Cambridge CB2 8BS, United Kingdom

One Liberty Plaza, 20th Floor, New York, NY 10006, USA

477 Williamstown Road, Port Melbourne, VIC 3207, Australia

314–321, 3rd Floor, Plot 3, Splendor Forum, Jasola District Centre,
New Delhi – 110025, India

79 Anson Road, #06–04/06, Singapore 079906

Cambridge University Press is part of the University of Cambridge.

It furthers the University's mission by disseminating knowledge in the pursuit of
education, learning, and research at the highest international levels of excellence.

www.cambridge.org
Information on this title: www.cambridge.org/9781108717328
DOI: 10.1017/9781108675918

© Pamela J. Stewart and Andrew Strathern 2019

First published 2019

A catalogue record for this publication is available from the British Library.

ISBN 978-1-108-71732-8 Paperback
ISSN 2397-9496 (online)
ISSN 2514-3786 (print)

Sacred Revenge in Oceania

Elements in Religion and Violence

DOI: 10.1017/9781108675918
First published: December 2018

Pamela J. Stewart
University of Pittsburgh

Andrew Strathern
University of Pittsburgh

ABSTRACT: Revenge is an important motivation in human affairs relating to conflict and violence, and it is a notable feature in both egalitarian societies and hierarchical societies within Oceania. In many of these societies revenge is traditionally a sacred duty to the dead whose spirits demand retributive action. Revenge is also sacred because it instantiates a norm of reciprocity in the cosmos, ensuring a balance between violent and quiescent sequences of action, marked by ritual. Revenge further remains an important hidden factor in processes of violence beyond Oceania, revealing deep human propensities for retaliatory acts and the tendency to elevate these into principles of legitimacy. Our study also explores ways in which sacred revenge is transcended through practices of wealth exchange.

KEYWORDS: sacred, revenge, Oceania, violence, reciprocity, warfare

ISBNs: 9781108717328 (PB), 9781108675918 (OC)
ISSNs: 2397-9496 (online), 2514-3786 (print)

Contents

Contents

Introduction

Revenge is a persistent motif in narratives of conflict. In state-based societies, and in monotheistic religious systems, its operation shifts from kin-based and interpersonal contexts to the imperatives of centralized orders of society. Kin-based revenge, previously seen as a sacred duty, then becomes devalued in favor of centralized processes. The societies we ourselves have directly worked with in Oceania developed another solution of their own by settling conflicts through payments of compensation for killings or accidental deaths, which over time could turn into positive ongoing exchanges of wealth items. Revenge was thus transformed into exchanges without the direct coercion of the state or an idea of a single powerful god, although in recent times it has been strongly inflected through encapsulation in state systems.

Revenge is a theme that has long been an important part of ethnographies on Pacific cultures, seen largely as a political phenomenon. By using the term "sacred" we draw attention to the deeper imperatives rooted in kinship, descent, reciprocity, balance, and ideas of the cosmos that underpin such practices. In the most immediate and pragmatic terms, revenge is important because it is declared to be demanded by the spirits of kin who have been killed in physical conflicts, and it is therefore sacred in that sense. In broader, but related, terms, revenge becomes a component of transcendent values in life, a central focus of such values, and thus also sacred, indefeasible, not to be questioned. Our narrative, however, also shows that such a value is not immutable, because physical revenge can be replaced by exchanges of wealth stemming from payments of compensation to stave off retaliatory action. Finally, taking the idea of the cosmos and a sense of balance within it as a part of the revenge complex, we also argue that retributive action to redress forms of wrongdoing or also environmental disruptions is a significant emergent feature of this complex and is therefore important in ways going well beyond contexts of political violence, extending into eco-cosmological contexts.

In this Element we focus mainly on Oceania, but it is important to recognize that the processes we discuss have been widespread in human history, and also that the imperative of revenge remains latent also in centralized political systems, appearing in the injunction not to take the law into one's own hands, but to leave it to the legal system or to the deity to encompass justice in the short or long run.

The history of revenge as a political theme is important throughout Oceania. It is found elsewhere, however, in epics dating from pre-state times, for example in Njal's saga, the epic of Gilgamesh, and Homer's two epics (the *Iliad* and the *Odyssey*). It is also the basis for stories that relate to early times of knights and warriors, and it is a powerful motif in narratives of historical conflict among the Maori population in New Zealand. Wherever ideas of honor are at stake, there combats to settle issues are likely to flourish. In Polynesian societal contexts, including the Maori, ideas of *tapu* intersected with ideas of revenge. An infringement of a *tapu* rule was an offense against a whole range of spatial rules and privileges and could lead to violent retaliation.

However, peace would depend on settling issues about the breaking of *tapu* rules or else in revenge retaliation. How broadly revenge was enacted was another important factor. Raymond C. Kelly made this point central to his discussion of the evolution of warfare in pre-state societies (Kelly 2000). His analysis was predicated on the idea that warfare is a collective political act of violence or physical force carried out in the name of the group, with responsibility therefore falling on the whole group. Collective responsibility means that retaliation for a killing may fall on any member of the group (or perhaps any adult male member, depending on how the matrix of violence is constructed).

Such an outgrowth from a narrow to a broader kin basis of calculating revenge could occur gradually over a number of generations, and we can find cases where the evolution to group responsibility and liability is in process but is not completed. In such cases an individual is always held responsible for starting a cycle of violence, and accordingly has to recruit help from group members and a network of related kin and allies in order either to wage further aggressive acts or to raise wealth items to pay compensation for an injury or killing already inflicted. There is, therefore, a combination of individual and collective criteria involved.

We will exemplify our argument in part with cases from places in the world where we have conducted research over many years, especially the Duna and Hagen areas of the Highlands of Papua New Guinea. While we deal directly with some processes of historical change, we are interested in setting up models of a small number of cases where the sacred revenge theme is found most clearly. The historical time of the descriptions depends on the times when the fieldwork was carried out and the materials published. We use ethnographies in which the theme is most clearly demonstrable and prominent. We do not suppose that these studies exhibit some ethnographic time zero, but they do represent times prior to substantial or sweeping exogenous changes, as for example when revenge activities were suppressed in Bellona Island by government action and Christian missionization (Kuschel 1998).

We have chosen a select number of cases that are paradigmatic for our theme. We do not aim at any comprehensive coverage in terms of the wider area of Oceania and its various subdivisions. In fact, it will be obvious that our cases come mostly from the South-West Pacific, with a focus on Melanesia. However, the importance of ideas about revenge is evident throughout the wider region, and our analyses here could be extrapolated *mutatis mutandis* to cases across the Pacific.

One type-case we have mentioned above comes from the ethnography of the Huli and Duna peoples of the Highlands of Papua New Guinea. The Huli and Duna both trace descent, and therefore eligibility for group membership, ambilineally or cognatically, meaning that membership may run through either male or female links, with some weight in terms of leadership tending to be placed on male or agnatic links. The ambilineal structure goes with a fluidity of recruitment of males for collective violence. In social contexts where there is great stress on agnatic lines, at least in ideological terms, collective responsibilities tend to be more defined, and the starting point for action becomes the group rather than an individual.

Regardless of such a difference in kin structures, revenge taking remains the norm until and unless the crucial move from killing to compensation is made. Moreover, the strongest motivation for seeking it remains at an individual or close kin level, feeding into the group solidarity. From the Hagen area in the Western Highlands Province of Papua New Guinea magical invocations, spoken at the time of going into battle in order to seek revenge, make this clear. A close relative of a man killed in fighting might invoke the ghost of his dead kinsman, telling the ghost to come and be at his elbow as he deploys a lance, or to sit on his eyebrows and nose and go ahead of him to assist in finding an enemy to kill. Close relatives were thus seen as those most immediately guided by revengeful ghosts into battle, emphasizing the sacred imperative to exact vengeance.

Such an imperative was not simply a rule or custom, to be followed out of a sense of duty or obligation. Instead, it was underpinned by emotions and by a sense of what the ghost of a killed relative would expect of its kinsfolk. The emotion was (and is) expressed in Hagen as *popokl*, a combination of frustration and anger, essentially a conative process impelling the person in one of two directions, either to take action to alleviate the *popokl* or to suffer it and fall sick as a result.

Popokl-induced sickness can be interpreted as a protest syndrome. *Popokl* is a dangerous, liminal state that can lead to sickness or to aggressive action on the part of the person who experiences it. *Popokl*, which is said to lodge in the person's *noman*, or mind, in Hagen conveys a sense of existential loss that goes with a sense of imbalance. *Noman* is both the seat of thought in general and the seat of the adjustment of the person to their social world. When the *noman* is well adjusted or "straight" (*kwun* in the Hagen Melpa language), the person's breath and their words flow easily from the chest to the mouth without any blockage. When the *noman* lies askew or blocked in the person (*peta ronom*), thoughts and judgment do not flow freely. To restore the person's emotional state to balance, either they must take redressive action or their sickness resulting from *popokl* has to be healed.

This emotional syndrome in Hagen finds its parallel in folk expressions widespread in Papua New Guinea about the effects of anger. The expression in Tok Pisin, a national lingua franca that grew out of early contacts with employees on coastal plantations and interactions among locals themselves, is *bel hat*, "hot stomach" or "hot insides," since *bel* in Tok Pisin covers all inside parts of the body. The opposite of *bel hat* is *bel kol*, "cool insides." Cool means calm, balanced. Hot means aroused or disturbed. *Bel hat* is the expected normal response to an injury, an insult, or the death of a kinsperson. Getting even by taking revenge is one means of cooling the insides. Where avenging a death is seen as a sacred activity required by dead spirits, we have the groundwork for a system of sacred revenge. However, the problem lies in what the processual outcomes are.

Bellona Island

A striking study that shows how far the ethic of revenge can go when it is not curbed or mediated by other values is the work by Rolf Kuschel on the small

Pacific island of Bellona in his book *Vengeance Is Their Reply: Blood Feud and Homicide in Bellona Island* (Kuschel 1998), one of a number of Polynesian Outlier islands in the Solomon Islands. The key to the remorseless pursuit of lethal vengeance on Bellona (Mungiki) is the concept of honor, linked to male-gendered values of strength, dominance, and concern not to be seen as weak. Kuschel argues that the reason why Bellonese men invariably sought to exact revenge for an insult or a killing was because not to do so would at once deplete their personal honor and diminish the standing of their kin group. The maintenance of honor was thus considered to be a prime social value, imbuing revenge with a sense of sacred value. The whole system was brought to a halt only by colonial control (Kuschel et al. 1999), accompanied by conversion to Christianity in 1938.

Torben Monberg's detailed ethnographic studies of Bellona rituals (Monberg 1991) clearly reflect the strong sense of honor that informed ideals of male personhood. Men might even get into conflict with the powerful Sky deities over issues to do with their honor, and these deities could also be capricious and hostile to humans when they felt slighted. Ancestors of particular groups were also seen as potentially pursuing causes of vengeance resulting from slights to their honor while they were alive.

In order further to understand the contextual basis of such a strong emphasis on honor and vengeance, while also explaining why this did not lead to the eventual demise of the groups as a whole through internecine killings, it will be useful to look at the ecology of the island and at the social exchanges of food that sustained positive relations among individuals and groups. Bellona is a small island, about 10 km long and 2.5 km in width on average, with high coral cliffs on its shorelines, and a high population density, based on its fertile interior soil. Settlements are mostly clustered in the interior. There were in the past three main groups, but one had become extinct. Group membership is traced patrilineally, and the highest rank is held by the agnatic male descendants of those ancestors who are commemorated as the original settlers. Genealogies of 24 generations were traditionally maintained in connection with this system of status. The various groups were (and probably still are) connected by ties of intermarriage, and affines were expected to engage in food exchanges. Indeed, the ethic of exchange, pervasive in Oceania, operated strongly in Bellona. At every feast, equal baskets of cooked food were given out to recipients, who then exchanged the baskets further as a means of strengthening social bonds in general and asserting a general equality among themselves. By contrast, however, we also know that people were very concerned about their relative status in the local lineage system being recognized, and this meant that there was an underlying structure of inequality that was both precariously maintained and vehemently insisted on.

All in all, it is apparent that Bellona, as a Polynesian outlier, somehow combines aspects of competitive leadership based on performance with hereditary status based on lineage seniority characteristic of chiefly systems. In this milieu, sacred revenge becomes hyper-emphasized, but it is also circumscribed. Revenge pertains only to men and particularly falls on men of high status. It can be exercised only against a killer or his close relatives (i.e., it cannot lead to war in Raymond Kelly's sense). Women cannot be killed in a revenge action. Given the fact that everyone is living in a crowded space and much effort has to be put into maintaining garden production and food distribution, there also has to be a method for peace-making after a round of homicides, and there was indeed an elaborate ritual of apology for killings that could be resorted to. As we have pointed out in an earlier publication, the step missing here is a linkage between gift exchange and conflict resolution, the crucial evolutionary step taken in the Papua New Guinea Highlands societies (Strathern and Stewart 2013).

"Payback" and Its Cosmic Implications

G. W. Trompf, in his insightful book *Payback* (Trompf 1991), has explored the ramifications of systems of revenge in parts of the South-West Pacific (Melanesia). Seeking for underlying shared features in the cultures of this region, Trompf developed the idea that "retributive logic" was a universal theme in the indigenous religious systems. Situating this theme in its historical context, Trompf notes that the incidence of fighting between groups may have increased as a result of epidemics of disease introduced by outside colonizers and traders (Trompf 1991, p. 26), and attributed to the sorcery of enemies, leading to vengeance raids. This pattern no doubt existed in some cases (see also Stewart and Strathern 2004). Inge Riebe (1991), for example, argued that the spread of witchcraft accusations among the Kalam people, who live on the northern edges of the Highlands of Papua New Guinea, was related to the dissemination of malaria into the Kalam area following its gradual spread southwards from lower-altitude areas in Madang Province as a result of early contact with outsiders.

Trompf notes (p. 25) that in discussing revenge killings he makes no distinction between feuding and warfare, because the ethic of revenge runs through all contexts of reciprocal violence. This is quite true. However, from another perspective, it is useful to bear this distinction in mind, because sacred revenge is transcended only when groups find an alternative way to maintain their reputations for strength, and this is achieved through group-based practices of compensation and exchanges of wealth flowing from these. A shift in practice of this kind also entails a shift in ideas of male personhood and a development of leadership based on exchange rather than on killing. Trompf refers to a statement that for the Chimbu people a heavy responsibility falls on the clansmen of any man whose killing has not been avenged: to carry out the act of revenge – or else? The implication is that failure to execute revenge is a failure in male or masculine identity, and that revenge is the only way to recover this identity and to re-balance the cosmos. The problem here is that the revenge killing will not necessarily be accepted by the other side as legitimately ending the sequence, so how can peaceful relationship ever be established? Because of the imperative to exact revenge, Trompf comments (p. 27) that "no Melanesian society could afford to shun violence" – unless, we may add, it found another way to express masculinity or a different definition of manhood itself. While in this Element we highlight the sacred character of revenge as a means of explaining its prevalence as a very costly form of social action, we also highlight the pathways by which revenge is transmuted into competitive exchange, taking Mount Hagen as our type-case.

A major purpose of Trompf's own discussion is to situate the meaning of revenge within the context of religion and to point out that this connection between religion and violence demands an "honest recognition" (p. 29). The invocation of "religion" here implies that the highest values of the society were tied up with revenge. An interesting exemplar follows in Trompf's text. He cites materials on the Gari people of Guadalcanal in the Solomon Islands, in which warriors tied knots in ropes to mark a symbolic strangling of their enemies, or they might cut up pieces of softwood, marking these as spears to kill named combatants. This kind of diversion into ritual symbolism suggests the pathways in which physical violence could be transformed into ritual violence. Trompf's next example (ibid.) shows this potentiality very clearly and directly resonates with data from all over the Highlands of Papua New Guinea. In Santa Ana, of the Eastern Solomon Islands, guests arriving for a ceremony by canoe were greeted by a set of armed and decorated men from the hosts, who would launch a mock ritual attack on them as a reminder of the potentiality of conflict and a *choice* not to engage in it (Trompf 1991, p. 30). Such ritualized challenges are a ubiquitous feature of compensations or peace-making events in the Highlands. In Hagen, for example, at a point where live pigs are going to be given away in the *moka* complex [wealth exchange complex] (see, e.g., Strathen and Stewart 2007, 2011), a selection of the male donors, highly decorated in costumes reminiscent of both warfare and social display in general, race down the line of pigs, calling out and stabbing the air with their spears, sometimes running into the pigs themselves, before gathering again at the head of the ceremonial ground to engage in the ritualized special speech form called *el ik*, "arrow talk," paradoxically associated with making peace (Strathern and Stewart 2000a).

Another example from our field areas can be drawn on here. Among the Wiru people of Pangia in the Southern Highlands Province, elaborate pig-killings were held in the1960s during early colonial times, involving gifts to partners who belonged to groups with whom they had been fighting in the recent past. Two practices of ritualized violence stood out on these occasions. Both inculcated the mode of killing pigs to be given away. In one act, a man killing a pig by clubbing its forehead would call out *Ne te moa*, "you get shit" – this to the intended recipient of pork from the pig. The term is an insult, and the pig being killed stands for the person who will receive the meat but is himself symbolically killed by the act of clubbing the pig. The second practice involved cutting up the pig to be given away in an unusual way. Instead of carving a pig into two longitudinal sides in the normative way, a donor would cut it crudely in half horizontally, so that its head and chest constituted one part and its rear the other. This was a representation of the recipient. What was ostensibly an act of friendship could equally be regarded as a continuation of hostility. In effect, such ritual acts encapsulated both alliance and enmity (see Strathern and Stewart 1999a, 2000b). We cannot establish whether such acts had a long time-depth or were recently established. In the context of recent pacification by the Australian Administration, it is, however, clear that ritualized forms of aggression of this kind belong to transitional phases of historical relations in which open fighting was suppressed but coded forms of ritual aggression entered into political relations. It is worth noting that the donors were the ones exercising ritual license. The recipients would come fully decorated, wearing headdresses and face-paint and holding a sheaf of arrows. They filed silently into the ceremonial space for the pig-killing and sat down very quietly. The donors first presented each male recipient with lengths of sugar-cane. They gave more such lengths to some men than to others. The recipients remained silent. The donors then proceeded to kill their pigs and cooked them. They gave cuts of pork for each length of sugar-cane given earlier. The women of the receiving group came forward from behind their menfolk and gathered up the pork into their capacious netbags and carried it off for consumption and distribution at home. There were no speeches made, in sharp contrast to the elaborate and formal *el ik* so prominent in Hagen. These Pangia events belong to a category of process in which physical killings were replaced by symbolic killings. The physical killing of the pigs marked the symbolic killing of the recipients. Yet, the presentation of pork negated pure hostility because a gift of pork was highly significant as a mark of friendship.

Among the Wiru, political alliance was never so fixed and clear as in Hagen. In warfare a group initiating a sequence of fighting might call on numerous helpers from a wide variety of nearby groups, forming a temporary coalition. Solid alliances between groups were not common, although in the 1960s people would identify historical friends and enemies, and even in the times of colonial pacification collective gifts between ex-enemies were not practiced. *Kange* payments [compensation gifts] as war-reparations were not expanded into ongoing exchanges of a *moka* type. Truncated alliance and transmuted sacred revenge therefore characterize the Pangia case as studied at that time in the 1960s onward.

To round out this example, we have earlier published two detailed accounts of a further elaboration of ritualized aggression among the Wiru. This was the building of a special ceremonial house for a pig-killing occasion in the village of Mamuane near the Poru river. The leader in this enterprise described it as a long-house in which donor families in the upcoming pig-kill had separate dwelling places and cooking hearths. The whole edifice was called a *Dapanda* and resembled styles found in neighboring areas where people lived in such long-houses on a permanent basis. There was a complex network of meanings built into the structure of the house, because the wood of its components carried messages about claims of dominance *vis-à-vis* the village's neighbors, who would be among those receiving pork at the pig killing. Like our other examples here, this case shows the plasticity of the imagination in producing ritualized versions of aggression that merge into alliance (Strathern and Stewart 2000b). Trompf refers to this sort of context as "the innuendo of inter-group antagonism" (Trompf 1991, p. 30).

Revenge and Sorcery-Divination

In cultural contexts in which any untoward death can be attributed to hostile action by some enemy, the question is bound to arise regarding who has caused the death of one's relative. Without such attribution, revenge cannot be carried out. Techniques of divination are instituted to find out the supposed attackers, if the death occurs outside of physical fighting. One technique is to attempt communication directly with the dead person's spirit, via the skull (mentioned by Trompf 1991 for the Mendi people of the Papua New Guinea Southern Highlands Province). Trompf also reports on the phenomenon of "payback running" among the Bena Bena of the Eastern Highlands of Papua New Guinea. After a person dies (a man in the example given), his spouse may become possessed by his spirit, which drives the one possessed to run frenetically from place to place as the ghost seeks to lead them to the sorcerer who caused the death. Clearly, this is based on the fundamental idea that the spirit wants revenge to be taken. Trompf notes that the possessed person may identify only the sorcerer's village, not the sorcerer in person. Also, if the village so identified is strong, revenge may be delayed. In other words, contingency modifies the determinacy of the sacred revenge motif, without, however, annulling it. When we say, with Trompf, that what is involved is religious action, it simply means that the spirit world is involved, and the spirits act exactly as the living do.

Trompf also refers to another practice, running with a divining pole, giving examples from Morobe Province in Papua New Guinea, specifically the Wantoat people. A ritual specialist would hold a length of bamboo and the dead spirit would energize it and make him run to the place of the killer.

This ritual practice was known also in two of our field areas, the Ialibu and Pangia areas of the Southern Highlands Province, where the divining stick was called *yomo kopini*. In this ritual, after a death, someone in the dead person's group would become possessed and the *yomo kopini* would lead them and others on a wild chase for the supposed killer-sorcerer. The description we have of this related to Ialibu, not Pangia, but the term used, *yomo kopini*, is in the Wiru language of Pangia, indicating that the custom was known there (Stewart and Strathern 2004).

Another area that we work in also used divining poles. This is the Duna area of Lake Kopiago (now in Hela Province, Papua New Guinea). Here the pole is called *ndele rowa*. It was decorated at one end with special nuts which would rattle as it was carried. An expert witch-finder took on the task of following the pole where the spirit led it, ideally to the house door of the supposed guilty witch, in which case the person identified as a witch (usually female) would be accused and compensation or the death of the "witch" be demanded. Sacred revenge or not, it is easy to realize that this method of divinatory identification could lead to further troubles (Stewart and Strathern 2002a). The Bena Bena principle of contingency is also likely to have applied.

A limitation of the concept of the sacred in relation to revenge or to warfare in general lies in the question of parity. Narrow revenge limits escalation of conflict, and also minimizes killings. An aggrieved dead spirit requires revenge for its own death, not the production of many more deaths. While citing payback running among the Bena as falling within the sacred revenge complex, Trompf also notes that Bena Bena warfare could involve driving enemies into refuge, taking over their land, burning down their residences, and killing all those who could not escape (Trompf 1991, p. 47). This scarcely seems to fit with sacred revenge as a re-balancing of the cosmos. It would be a mistake, then, in our view, to try to subsume all of warfare under sacred revenge. In his theoretical approach, Trompf insists on a holistic approach that does not separate politics and economics from religion; but was it religion that precipitated the Bena into general acts of conquering other groups, and taking over their land?

Other data indicate a sacred character in social practices requiring the killing of others, most notably in the context of head-hunting. An example cited by Trompf (p. 52) comes from the Marind-Anim people of West Papua. The Marind-Anim sought to take the heads of enemy groups and then used the names of their victims to name a cohort of their own children. Thus, naming was tied inextricably to killing others. This custom may have been sacred, then, but it was not apparently based on revenge as such, and in what way was the practice connected to balancing the cosmos? Trompf concludes his own argument by saying that it is blood-letting histories that explain why the extremes of warfare "so often prevail over pressures for compensation" (p. 54). In most of his examples, however, the question of compensation does not enter, revenge simply taking central place. An alternative approach is to start by looking at possibilities for compensation, a theme we will return to shortly.

Trompf continues his investigation by citing cases in which deities or spirits of ancestors were involved as sponsors of revenge activities, including an intriguing but obscure narrative about an idol hidden in a cave among the Tauade (a Goilala group in central Papua) which had to be approached each yam harvest time and re-blackened while being asked for help in warfare. In the Wahgi area (now Jiwaka Province, formerly a part of Western Highlands) Trompf cites the prehistoric mortars and pestles that were found and incorporated into war magic rituals (Trompf 1991, pp. 58, 60). These stones were called *kukoinamb*, *ku* being a general term for stone.

It is interesting to reflect here that such stones, widely used in ritual contexts throughout the Highlands, were in the neighboring Hagen area west of the Wahgi central features in ritual practices not connected to warfare but to the periodic celebration of great acts of veneration towards a Female (*Amb Kor*) or Male spirit (*Kor Wöp*), having to do with human and environmental fertility, but not warfare (Stewart and Strathern 2002b, 2002c; Strathern and Stewart 1999b, 2004a). The example shows that indigenous "religion" may contain complex features, both ones connected to warfare and ones connected to peaceful aims.

Where Wahgi ideas overlap significantly with ones from the Hagen area is in the sphere of ideas about sorcery and witchcraft, in the context of enduring enmity between kin groups. The term *kum* can be used in the Wahgi area both for hostile sorcery against enemies and for witchcraft power. A sorcerer, *kumyi*, may try to wreak havoc on their enemies by bringing *kum* substances close to their settlement. The enemies' own sorcerers may find this and turn it against their foes in warfare. They bring the *kum* into the battlefield, and it will now act to identify the sorcerer who planted it and make him vulnerable to being killed in battle. There is no direct equivalent of this use of kum in Hagen, where war magicians and war magic were seemingly less intense than among the Wahgi groups. In Hagen, also, ordinary sorcery substances were described as *kopna*, not *kum*, but the same structured fears surrounded sorcery suspicions in both areas. Men feared that wives who were in-married from other groups might bring hostile sorcery stuff in to kill someone in their husband's group, if not the husband himself. A woman's inclination to do this or not would depend on the relationship with her husband's group and on pressures brought to bear on her by her natal group. There was always a risk that a woman from an enemy group might be tempted to act on behalf of her kinsfolk in this way, thus becoming an agent of sacred revenge on their behalf but risking her own life severely in doing so. This was because such a woman was a prime target of suspicion in the case of a death. Two consequences followed. First, there was a disinclination to marry between groups that were major enemies. Second, there was no means to establish innocence for a woman in the case of being accused, any more than there was any easy proof of their guilt.

Another usage of the term *kum* in the Wahgi area was *kum koimp*, translatable as witchcraft or *tanguma* in the Tok Pisin lingua franca of Papua New Guinea. *Kum koimp* is an especially disturbing notion, linked in Hagen at least to phases of time when people feared that witchcraft was on the increase and that female cannibal witches were breaking into recently established graves of the dead, exhuming them and eating their flesh (see Stewart and Strathern 2004). Phases of moral and psychological panic of this kind tend to correspond with social stresses in times of rapid change, and to spread through accelerated rumors. Recently, since about 2014, another phase of intensified concern about witchcraft has set in, also linked to a period of intense social change, commodification, and widespread popular discontent with corruption in political and business contexts. Such fears of witchcraft go together with ongoing fears of sorcery attacks, sometimes coming from within the community rather than from remote enemies.

The general point here is that ideas about sorcery and witchcraft stem from both old and new hostilities between groups and over gendered issues.

Trompf illustrates this point with reference to "stone bird" sorcery in the Mendi area (Southern Highlands Province). A sorcerer is said to carry around a prehistoric stone effigy of a bird and direct it to exercise spirit power to kill a victim. Such a sorcerer would be hired by an aggrieved group to carry out a revenge killing by this means, thus constituting an act within the sacred revenge complex. In Mendi, sorcery techniques, however, could also be used to retaliate against an offending exchange partner or a sexual rival, perhaps from within the community. This process might be accelerated by changes in patterns of movement following colonial control, as we have documented for the Pangia area (Southern Highland Province) at a stage of colonial and post-colonial history (Stewart and Strathern 2004). And new varieties of sorcery have also been introduced into and spread throughout the Papua New Guinea Highlands as a result of the construction of roads and trucks travelling on them from the coast to the interior and vice versa. These developments in ideas about sorcery all feed on the historical legacy of processes of sacred revenge that held in the past and were suppressed through colonial power, as also by post-colonial governments intent on modernization and missionization as paths to the future. At local levels, further, leaders might use the prevalence of fears of sorcery by claiming to hire the most powerful sorcerers to act on their side and to use these powers to increase their influence in comparison with their rivals. We see here a twist or inflection of the sacred revenge motif, with "big-men" harnessing it to increase their own local power.

Another example, from the Mekeo area of Papua, is pointed to by Trompf. In pre-colonial times senior chiefs of lineages controlled the activities of sorcerers. Missionaries and government brought villages together and consolidated their increased size. Chiefs lost control, and sorcerers gained in influence. More people became known as sorcerers, envy between families arose because of inequalities in the betel-nut trade, and sorcery suspicions proliferated. A process of this kind shows clearly the degeneration of a ritually sanctioned and directed structure of sacred revenge into a fluid terrain of uncertain suspicions and rampant fears stemming from new social inequalities and the loss of power of chiefs, along with the rise of a different kind of self-made leaders opportunistically seeking power by claiming influence over the activities of sorcerers. Trompf's analysis of these negative events portrays a bleak picture, indeed, of the deleterious effects of colonial control and post-colonial economic trends. Did the sacred, then, go out of revenge, and what took its place?

We will go back now to the Mount Hagen case in pursuit of the historical line that leads from revenge to exchange, at least for this society, but also for others as Trompf's own next chapter in his comprehensive review documents, beginning with the Wahgi people, neighbors of the Hageners (Trompf, p. 97).

The Genesis of Exchange: Mount Hagen

Given an underlying historical ethic valorizing revenge as an imperative, sanctioned by the putative wishes of dead kinsfolk killed in fighting or supposedly killed by sorcery, what would induce a shift away from revenge into the offering and acceptance of compensation?

First, there has to be present an idea of compensation itself. This idea must be calibrated exactly in terms of cultural values. The facilitating element here is the notional equivalence between humans and pigs as valuables that can be offered in place of them. If there is no idea of commutability between pigs or other items as wealth and aspects of value in human lives, there is no cultural groundwork for making compensation payments. In most places in the Highlands of Papua New Guinea, pigs were already given great value as media of sacrifice to ancestral kin, so gifts of pigs were easily thought of as sacrifices or potential sacrifices of this sort. Gift-giving as compensation begins, then, with sacrifice in this sense.

Second, ideas about the body are involved and about injuries done to it. Physical violence in conflicts occurs within local residential groups, and the first claim made by an injured person or their immediate kin is to ask that their "blood be put back" or put in place again. The phrase in the Melpa language is *mema pindi*. Blood, one of the vital constituents of the body, should remain inside the skin. If it flows out of the skin, it is "matter out of place," to adapt Mary Douglas's famous characterization of cultural ideas about "dirt" or "pollution" (Douglas 1966). The Melpa phrase here recognizes this starting point. It specifies further that the life force of the person who has been injured has been weakened and made vulnerable. In order to strengthen it again and to enlist the support of their dead kin in the fight to replace vitality, a pig is required. Within the group this is done quickly, so as, by the same act, to restore social relations and appease the anger (*popokl*) of the person harmed. In ethnopsychology terms, *popokl*, as we have noted above and in previous publications, is socially dangerous (see, e.g., Strathern and Stewart 2010). It can lead to further acts of retaliatory violence, which would be harmful within the group. It can also lead to sickness among those who are experiencing it, requiring further sacrifices to ask dead kin to help the person recover. All in all, it is axiomatic that a gift should be offered and accepted in order to put back the blood (life force) of the injured and open the way to further conciliatory acts.

The model or plan for inter-group compensation is thus found in the small-scale in-group context as we have just sketched it. Why, however, would it be extended beyond this level?

Here, social structure and history must be invoked. The life-world of the Hageners consisted of two different axes of social relations. One was the inner dimension of those related by descent and by intermarriage. The other was the outer dimension of long-term hostility with major enemies. Relations with the latter were marked by an alternation between avoidance and armed combat along boundaries, whenever such boundaries were violated or suspicions of specific acts of sorcery commanded attention. Intermarriage was not compatible with such a complex. With the former category of people, there was frequent intermarriage and even some pattern of expected reciprocity described, from a male viewpoint, as *amb aklwa etemen*, "they customarily exchange women." Marriage entailed the payment of bridewealth in pigs and shell valuables, accompanied by return gifts as an endowment for the bride. The pigs given by the groom's kin to the bride's people were (and are) described as *penal kng*, "pigs of the open area," where the term *penal* refers notionally to the same cleared space of a ceremonial ground on which bigger presentations of gifts were made, taking the form of compensation payments. The endowment pigs, which went with the bride to the place of her husband, to be looked after by her, were known as *mangal kng*, "the pigs of the house," referring to the fact that the new bride would look after them in her woman's house and have them as breeding stock to build up a herd. Some, at least, of the *penal kng*, pigs of the open ground or plaza, might be cooked and their meat distributed to natal kinsfolk of the bride. The *penal kng* were the part of the overall bridewealth gifts that acted as a compensation or replacement for the bride herself as she was removed from her natal place and went in virilocal marriage to the husband's place. We see inscribed in bridewealth, then, a cultural schema isomorphic with compensation payments for killings. Indeed, a part of the traditional bridewealth was called *peng pokla*, pigs to "cut off the head of the bride," not in any literal sense, but as a marker that her personhood, or "head," was being severed from her natal kin and taken to her husband's group. Bridewealth in this sense was metaphorically like head-hunting in warfare among other Papua New Guinean groups (not practiced in Hagen). The difference, of course, was that the bridewealth did not involve killing but was actually the beginning of new life processes mediated by the exchange of pigs as wealth.

In terms of the analyses developed earlier for social structure in Hagen, there was a clear categorical distinction between minor enemies, with whom the group also intermarried (*el öninga*, "small arrow"), and major enemies, with whom intermarriage was avoided (*el parka*, "red bird of paradise arrow"), and from whom both sorcery attacks and open physical combat was expected. Further, minor enemies were expected to be one's allies in conflict with major enemies, and from this dovetailing or overlap in relations came the categories of compensation that could be enacted. There could be direct compensation for killings in minor fights between *el öninga* people. Or there could be what was in fact a favorite practice known as "dead man" (*kui wuö*), meaning a payment of compensation to an allied group when an ally had been killed in warfare with a major enemy. If there was a sacred duty to take revenge on major enemies, concentrating on a killer or this person's close kin, then there arose an equally sacred imperative to re-balance relations with allies by giving them wealth that they could use to replace the one they had lost. In these cases the principles are always the same. A death must be balanced by either another death or by a presentation of wealth to assuage justifiable *popokl* or to enable new life to be created by the deployment of wealth. In this regard, the over-lapping of minor enmity and inter-marriage creates the strategic space in which hostility is transmuted into peace-making. The axiom "death requires revenge" is shifted into the axiom "death requires new life," and this requirement is met, symbolically or actually, by saying that a gift of wealth paid in reparation to allies is called "carrying the man," or "bearing the man," where the verb in the Melpa language refers both to the simple act of carrying something, such as a pig trussed up as a sacrificial gift, and to the act of giving birth to ("bearing" in this sense) a child. The major ally payment known as *wuö metemen*, "they carry the man," depends for its sense on the notion that the wealth given can be used to form a bridewealth payment for a new bride who will be expected to bear children for the group. Hence the meaning of wealth is "life-giving material."

As explained in earlier publications (e.g., Strathern 1971 [2007]; Strathern and Stewart 2000a), a large-scale payment of this kind would be built up to only over a period of time and would require much effort and commitment, reaffirming the alliance in question. There was in the past a sequence of minor transactions that might lead to such a large-scale payment, beginning with one called *wantep kan kng ngoromen*, "they give the pig of the *wantep* tree-bark." The meaning of this term was that a small live pig (*kng elyip*) would be bound with tree-bark stripped from a fast-growing fallow tree, the *wantep*, and carried over directly by an emissary to the resentful and grieving kin of the dead man as an immediate appeasement and an instrument of ameliorating their *popokl* that might lead them to seek revenge. After that, other gifts might be made, building up to the final reparation gift. Here, too, there were complications because one-way gifts shifted into two-way exchanges by means of a further mechanism. This mechanism worked only because of affinal ties between the actors involved. To help the donor group find the wealth needed to make the upcoming gift, the expecting recipients would themselves give some pigs in advance, thus assisting to finance the big event.

Historical Complications in the Revenge Complex

We see here a threefold shift out from the sacred revenge complex, in which, however, the central motif is preserved. This motif is the value of a life, realized in payments flowing from death:

1. A killing generates a response of killing in retaliation, thus a life for a life.
2. A killing generates a response by way of a payment of wealth, thus wealth for a life.
3. The prospective recipients of (2) make an initial payment to the donors, thus wealth for wealth.

Throughout this sequence the unique value of a human life lost in conflict remains the enduring "sacred" motif. The edges of this kind of sequence mark the boundaries of alliance versus enmity between the groups involved. Between major enemies the ethos of sacred revenge remains paramount, but it is precisely here that complications set in with pacification, colonial, and post-colonial government control. The history of groups within two neighboring council areas in the Western Highlands Province of Papua New Guinea clearly shows an expansion of scale in sacred revenge in the context of colonial control and development and attempts to deal with such changes in the scale of social relations. This is the history of Mul and Dei councils during the 1960s and 1970s.

A more detailed account appears in our 2011 study, *Peace-Making and the Imagination* (Strathern and Stewart 2011, drawing on earlier sources). Here, only points relevant to the discussion of sacred revenge will be drawn out. In setting up local Government Councils in the Highlands in the 1960s, the Australian Administration was aiming to contribute to self-governance for the local tribes and to expand the size of political groupings in doing so. Within one such Council area, Dei Council, the tribes formed into two major opposed blocs: the paired alliance of the Kombukla and Minembi tribes and the smaller paired alliance of the Tipuka and the Kawelka tribes. These alliance groups were major enemies of each other, while within each alliance minor enmities and exchanges of wealth took place. In the neighboring Mul council a similar structure prevailed between two major groups, the Kumndi and the Nengka, with the Remndi people sandwiched between them. As Councils, Mul and Dei operated quite separately.

They were, however, brought together into a single further level of political structure for the election of a representative to the recently established House of Assembly, the forerunner of the national Parliament that was established after Papua New Guinea became an independent state in September 1975. The Australian Administration decided to contrive this amalgamation out of an ideology of enlarging the scales of political consciousness in a way that was considered appropriate to the modern, developing nation-state that was envisaged for the near future. There was also already an aim to bring the two Councils together into a single Council, but this produced a backlash, at least in the Dei Council. How could this have been otherwise? Two very new levels of structure were being arbitrarily introduced into a kin-based societal context founded on the exercise of influence through exchanges of wealth emerging from compensation payments to make peace. The Council structure was the first level of novelty, and the election for a House of Assembly Member was a further level. Elections by voting process were entirely new concepts also. A kin-based structure was bound to prevail through all this recent change, but who could perceive what the future would be?

The two Councils, Mul and Dei, were like super-tribes deliberately set up in competition with each other. They were separate, and the more so because of the recent creation of them as different administrative Councils. They were like major enemy groups rather than minor enemy allies.

How, then, did all this play out in the next several years? A complex revenge situation interposed itself into the electoral competition. In Dei, the dominant candidate was from the Tipuka-Kawelka alliance. In Mul, the leading candidate was from the small Remndi group bordering Dei and was able to secure votes from both of the major tribes in this Council, the Kumndi and the Nengka. On October 8, 1967, a Nengka driver of a truck going through Dei struck an old man of a small clan of the Minembi tribe of Dei, the Yelipi clan. The man's kinsfolk attacked the driver and caused his death from head wounds.

A crisis emerged. In the past the issue would have been dealt with through the immediate clans involved. But now Dei and Mul had been created as new political groups, and as rivals they were forced into competition over a new source of power and prestige relating to the as yet non-existent but soon-to-be independent nation of Papua New Guinea. So, what to do? An extremely interesting event ensued. Councilors of Dei came together as a new unity with no previous basis. Both large and small groups agreed to contribute to a general payment coming from the whole Dei Council that would go to the Nengka as a compensation for the driver's death. They also agreed that the small clan of those who had attacked the driver would in addition pay a number of pigs and shell valuables as a marker of their special responsibility. A main aim of this move was to forestall a likely effort at justifiable (sc. sacred) revenge on the part of the Nengka, and this might have fallen on anyone of Dei Council as the Councils were really thought of as super tribes. Such a revenge would plausibly be seen as "sacred revenge" by the Nengka. The other leading reason was to try to maintain some goodwill between the Councils and allow the election process to continue, as it did. The Dei candidates were afraid to campaign in Mul, and one of the present authors (AJS) was prevailed on to take the leading Dei candidate on a somewhat hazardous drive through Mul for some brief stops. Mul Council had a higher population also, and the two Mul candidates were from the same small Remndi tribe and not in serious contention. One of the Mul candidates won, leaving all in Dei Council disappointed, and further making reconciliation between the Councils impossible (Stewart and Strathern 2002d).

Worse was to follow. On the border between Mul and Dei there had been an arrangement to set up a new rural police post that would serve people in both Councils. The place was in the territory of the Mul candidates in the election. It was also close to the home of the clansmen of the truck driver who had been killed in Dei: a dangerous, liminal place indeed. Peripheral places and groups sometimes move unexpectedly into the center of action. The Nengka clan, the Kuklanggil, that was involved in the issues here was small and had migrated away from the main Nengka tribal complex to live near the Dei border. The Minembi Yelipi clan group of Dei were also migrants and refugees from ancient warfare who had settled among the Kombukla-Minembi tribal bloc, the opposite bloc to the Tipuka-Kawelka. (Their name indicates that their origins lie far south of Dei in the Ialibu area.) Isolated groups like these can seek exaggerated ways to recover prestige or assert themselves. Thus, the Minembi Yelipi clan caused a political upheaval that permanently altered the political situation of Mul and Dei. Internally, the result was to strengthen a sense of solidarity in Dei itself, centered on the figure of their leading politician. The crisis already practically guaranteed this politician's prominence for the future. What happened next pushed this process further, while almost ending his life.

The politician decided to attend the opening of the new border police post. He did not take any elaborate set of bodyguards with him and his decision to attend was taken in spite of various omens and dream warnings that he might be attacked and killed, including the theft of an eagle kept in a cage at his settlement that was clearly a symbol of the politician himself. At the event an assailant from the Nengka Kuklanggil clan rushed at him wielding an axe and cut him severely on the face with a blow clearly designed to kill him. He survived, however, and was rushed to a hospital in Hagen town and thence to the national capital, Port Moresby, where he spent a long time recovering, and on return received an emotional greeting from hundreds of supporters. The assailant, who was a man of low status (and perhaps had been successfully persuaded by his clan leaders to attempt the assassination with a promise of a reward), was captured and put on trial in Mount Hagen. One of the present authors (AJS) visited the Dei politician regularly while he was being treated in the hospital, and later he also served as the translator in the Supreme Court hearing on the attempted killing, since the accused knew no English and the expatriate trial judge declared he required a competent translator from the local Melpa language into English, rather than the lingua franca Tok Pisin.

The result of the trial was that the attacker received a jail sentence of ten years. Why did he launch such an attack, fraught with risk to himself and his group? Sacred revenge seems to be the answer, even though compensation had been offered and taken for the earlier killing. The Kuklanggil paid a further price. A joint "Trouble Committee" of both Mul and Dei determined that they should be removed from their land at the border and re-settled elsewhere. In general, this case history shows the ongoing powerful effects of cultural notions extending into "modern" political history. The same conclusion can be found from the continuing fears and accusations of sorcery focused on business and political leaders, who are said to provoke jealousy on the part of rival groups and individuals and therefore to be targets for removal by clandestine administration of lethal substances.

Mul and Dei were split back into two constituencies and never joined again. In subsequent years, further conflicts along tribal lines disturbed the lives of the Kawelka people in Dei, and in late 2017, when we made a tour through Mul, we observed large areas that were devastated and left unpopulated following years of severe conflict between major groups there. The sacred revenge mentality has re-entered life, it appears, and left its mark on the land itself, more than forty years after 1975, when Papua New Guinea became an independent nation-state.

Peace-Making in Hagen: A Reprise in Ongka's Account

The Kawelka leader, Ongka-Kaepa, describes in his autobiography a circumstance in which a death was likely to lead to revenge activity. The death of an important man would lead to a suspicion that this had been caused by sorcery coming from traditional enemies. Ongka notes that an elaborate funeral for the leader would be instituted and his body placed high on a platform (*paka*). Then, says Ongka, one of his close kin, such as a son, might begin to shake as the dead man's spirit putatively possessed him and started to indicate what group had made the sorcery that killed him.

An episode of this kind was actually recorded in the filming of *Ongka's Big Moka* in 1974 (AJS was the anthropologist who worked to make the film with a filmmaker at the time), and it led to a set of threats that disrupted the *moka* (exchange) that Ongka was planning to make to his allies among the Tipuka tribe. As he explains in the film, Ongka did his utmost to keep the situation from erupting into open warfare, and in this he succeeded, partly because this was happening in 1974, only a year before Papua New Guinea's Independence in 1975.

Ongka describes in another part of his story how war was conducted in his youth, and later how peace could be put in place (Strathern and Stewart 1999c). Ongka first describes minor hostilities with sticks as weapons that took place between minor enemies within the tribe or with allied clans of the pair-group of tribes (Kawelka and Tipuka). Compensation payments resulting from such combats were called *mongaemb*, he notes. (Our Melpa Dictionary has this as *mongamp rui*, thus employing a slightly different dialect form, from the Central Melpa area, with the translation "making atonement" for the sake of "reconciliation"; see Stewart, Strathern, and Trantow 2011.) Sacred revenge did not apply in this context. The aim was to reinstate friendship.

Ongka gives a much more violent account of major conflicts, and the roles of allies in these, as well as the destruction of houses and the rape of women of the enemy group. Allies, he notes, would take it on themselves to protect the women of their allied groups, keeping them safe from abuse of this kind, and receiving grateful payments of pork in return when the battle was over. Ongka gives a dramatic account of the large gifts of pork to allies, piled up on high, he says, until the heaps reached as high as the bird of paradise headdresses worn by the visiting recipients.

Ongka's account has details from his first-hand experiences. He notes that for serious fights they built a special communal men's house called *el klaka manga*. (The term *klaka* refers to the fact that the house was separated off from the ordinary settlements in the clan area.) They would meet in this house to make sacrifices and prayers for their dead kin to help them win in fighting. When the fighting was finished, Ongka explains, they would dismantle the house, but they put the center post in a swampy area and lifted it back out when they were ready to reward their allies and said that they would raise it like a funeral platform for the ancestral spirits (*kor paka*) and make gifts to the allies.

He returns to the topic of revenge. In addition to observing the process whereby a kinsman of someone who had died by sorcery might be said to become possessed by the dead person's spirit and identify the sorcerer, they would at times bury the body close to the surface of the ground, so that the spirit could easily come out and help them to get revenge. Later, after the flesh had decomposed, they gathered the bones, including the head, and put them in a "spirit house" (*kor manga*) and made sacrifices of pork to it, and called out to all the ancestral spirits, male and female, to come and eat and then protect them in their next round of fighting to get revenge. A man would especially single out a pig's head for dedication to his dead father's spirit and would pray for the spirit's protection so as not to die by sorcery or by spear or arrow or by an accident.

> You . . . come and stand straight in front of me
> Come and be at my lips and at my eyebrows
> Eat this head
> And help me.
>> (Strathern 1979, p. 53); Strathern and Stewart 1999c)

(The spirits were spoken of as consuming the meat of the sacrifice by smelling the rich aroma [*tindeklem*] of it when it was removed from the earth oven.)

Ongka's Account Continued

If revenge was obtained, they would say that their dead kin had helped them, and they would dance, decorate, and say that now they were going to cook and eat their enemy whom they had killed. Ongka notes that they did not actually eat the body, but the symbolism indicates the sense of dominance conveyed by the expression. In the Melpa language the expression is *wuö kaemb kaklk noromen*, "they roast and eat the man's liver," the liver being a marker of strength and a repository of the vital humor of blood (see Stewart and Strathern 2002c on this). The liver is symbolically removed in this expression, implying the person's death and destruction of their identity.

Ongka's vivid account of actual sequences of fighting gives a startling insight into the ways that groups and their leaders manipulated structural relations and bribes, as well as imputations of sorcery in justification of their fights. As well, it provides a running commentary on collateral violence against women who were not targets for killing so much as targets for rape when one group swept over the territory of another. Most of his narrative has to do with the sphere of what we have called "minor enemies." He makes it clear that killings and rapes were a part of the conflicts, and that at times the Kawelka (his group) were hard pressed to survive at all. And the account also makes clear that some of the fiercest fights were with neighbors of the Kawelka, the Oklembo clan of the Tipuka tribe, a paired clan of the Kitepi clan. We see here the replication of political relations at different levels. Oklembo and Kitepi were paired, but the Kawelka's main alliance was with the Kitepi, because the territory they gained as asylum seekers included some Kitepi land, and marriages were set up to strengthen ties. The Oklembo lived a bit further away, with less intermarriage. In 1964 onwards, with plans for elaborate *moka* events that led to Ongka's big moka of 1974, this difference in clan relations was still evident and affected the standing of a small group of Kawelka whose settlement was an enclave in Oklembo territory. Again, this pattern was mitigated by a single marital alliance with the daughter of an Oklembo leader.

Another feature of Ongka's account here is that he makes no mention of death compensation payments between the enemies in fighting. Instead – and this is the classic feature found also in the case of the Tsembaga Maring group studied by Roy Rappaport (Rappaport 1968) – Ongka stresses how in spite of all the violent actions, the combatants would eventually tire of the privations and insecurity and losses of life, and so would agree to make peace. The purpose of the peace-making was to reward their allies generously with large amounts of cooked pork. He refers to peace-making more in the manner of a long truce. After violence all round, "Now there is no quarrel between us, let us separate and be quiet" (Strathern 1979, p. 61). He adds that both sides gradually rebuilt their settlements and raised pigs, for about four years. Then they made the reparations to their respective helpers, with elaborate speeches of thanks and foregrounding how their friends had protected the Kawelka wives against wartime rape as well as assisting in the actual fighting. The reparations here were made, again as with the Maring, to ensure continued help in the future. The speeches were important ways in which memories were created, fixed, and tied to events, encapsulating much detailed local knowledge of places and actions. This knowledge would be greatly at risk of being lost over time, and with it much relevant information on political history. Speeches kept rationales for revenge alive, as well as accounts of exchanges made to create friendship. Ongka was himself an oral archive of such knowledge, and with his death in 2003 much of this archive would have been lost, and with it the incentives for keeping ideas of revenge alive. As long as memories existed, however, and reconciliation had not taken place, there was a strong tendency to wait until an opportunity to take revengeful action arose. In another passage Ongka noted (Strathern 1979, p. 56) that in narratives they do not mention names, for fear of stirring up revenge feelings. He added (ibid.): "Actually people know, and they don't forget, they will wait a long time to obtain their revenge."

While one might get the impression that fighting was the main pre-occupation prior to pacification by the Australian Administration, starting in the 1930s, Ongka's next chapter goes on to make it clear how wealth acquisition in pigs and shells was very important. A particular man, the *moka*-maker, cleared the ceremonial ground, built a men's house, decorated its central post, and eventually, with his supporters, laid out rows of pearl shells as a *moka* gift. On the climactic occasion the chief donor made an impressive (and aggressive) rush up the ceremonial ground, decorated in black charcoal and holding an adze in one hand prior to making his speech. We see here the transmutation of hostility into gift-giving, which makes the shift from revenge to exchange.

In another chapter Ongka also provides an unusual account of a ritual of peace-making prior to making reparation gifts to allies. He starts from the point he has earlier mentioned, a time when people were tired of a sequence of fighting. The ritual was called removing *el pint pint*. The first step was to put barriers of leaves across the paths used by warriors to invade the home territory. The leaves included cordylines, ritual markers of boundaries and limits that would take root and exist after the other leaves had rotted away. Anyone who broke these barriers would be rebuked for spoiling the peace. In other words, a ritual *tapu* (in the Melpa language *mi*) was placed on hostile activity, allowing the group to work hard and produce gardens for feeding pigs and breeding numbers of them.

After about three years it was time to perform the ritual. They said that any crop failures were due to *el pint pint*, and they dressed up a tall man in charcoal and white and yellow stripes, wearing a gourd mask and carrying an old spear covered in soot. They took vegetable foods to a big ceremonial men's house built for warfare. An expert bespelled decorative leaves to hang around the house and bring back fertility. Calling the man covered in dry charcoal as though they were bringing him as a spirit down from the sky above, they enumerated all kinds of "dry" things he wore, and then ritually chased him to their land boundary across the path of war near a big river (the Mökö river, running through Kawelka and Tipuka territory). The youths of the group killed pigs in sacrifice to the ancestors invisibly witnessing this ritual transition, and then everyone removed the barriers on the pathway, now that the figure representing warfare had been driven out.

Now they cooked all the vegetables taken up to the old war house, soft, fertile foods, and they distributed one sweet potato to each participant to feed to their pigs and make them grow big. After some further time had passed, they would make their large gifts of pork to their allies.

Maring and Melpa: From Elementary to Complex Structures

The work of Roy Rappaport, Andrew Vayda, William Clarke, and Ed LiPuma on the Maring people of the Schrader Ranges in the northern part of the Highlands of Papua New Guinea made these people very well known in the ethnographic literature from the 1960s onward. Major arguments between scholars arose out of controversies regarding the putative ecological functions of warfare. These need not detain us here, except to say that the major ritual cycle that Rappaport (Rappaport 1968) describes from the time of his first fieldwork there, the *kaiko* pig-killing festival, deeply involves its participants in ecological relationships with their environment, by way of their use of resources for the *kaiko*. So, the ritual cycle is certainly also an ecological cycle, not just with regard to the pigs that are raised for sacrificing but also in relation to garden crops, wild plants and creatures, and from the Maring viewpoint the spirits that occupy the lower-altitude areas and those of the high mountain tops, headed by the powerful Smoke Woman, the Female Spirit (*kun kaʒe ambra*) (Strathern and Stewart 2001). The whole Maring ecology of living is bound up, in Rappaport's account, with a geographical cosmos balancing low valley ground and high mountain tops. The "red" ancestral spirits that are said to demand revenge for their deaths in warfare are also in the mountain domain of the Smoke Woman, and shamans are the ones who get into communication with her as preparations for the *kaiko* proceed. Clansmen carry ripe red pandanus fruits grown in sacred groves. Two men raise the fruits high and carry them around, and the group makes a chant to the Smoke Woman, offering the fruits to her and calling the names of high mountain tops said to be habitats of the Spirit. After this, the fruits are steamed in special earth ovens. Pigs dedicated to the "red spirits" and the Smoke Woman are cooked in ovens constructed above ground, and those for the lower environment spirits go into an earth oven dug into the ground (Rappaport 1968, p. 177).

These brief details are excerpted from Rappaport's account in order to give some idea of the complex ecological symbolism that pervades the whole ritual process. The basic underpinnings of this process are as follows:

1. When a bout of fighting is over, clansmen take red cordyline plants and plant these at the boundaries of their territories. The cordylines contain the men's life force and are called *yu min rumbim*, "men's souls' cordylines." As long as the cordylines remain planted in the ground, there can be no fighting.

2. The clan families spend numbers of years making gardens, raising pigs, and preparing to be ready for killing these pigs in the *kaiko* festival and offering them to the red spirits as a mark of their solemn intention to avenge their deaths in sacred revenge.

3. The clan invites allies in the last bout of warfare to come and receive pork for their help in warfare. They complete a year-long range of rituals leading up to the pig kill. They uproot the cordylines and prepare for war after they have gifted large amounts of pork to pay their allies.

4. The group enters into warfare again to achieve vengeance on behalf of the red spirits. Smoke Woman is invited to be on their side in this phase. Uprooting the *rumbim* is a fiduciary or irrevocable sign that the group will enter into a phase of sacred revenge on behalf of the red spirits. There may be tactical delays in this process, but the whole *kaiko* is (or was prior to colonial pacification in the early 1960s) a combination of divinatory and promissory rituals indicating that the cosmic process of revenge taking will be entered into, beginning with the uprooting of the *rumbim*. That the *kaiko* is a preliminary to the resumption of warfare is marked by its division into two phases, *wobar* and *de*. *Wobar* is the name of the songs sung on entering into an early phase of fighting (the "nothing fight," Rappaport 1968, p. 182) and *de* marks the song warriors sing on entering into the more lethal "axe fight" (ibid.) Many other ritual sequences that Rappaport delineates in detail signify the process of moving towards fighting again. For example, magic fighting stones that were hanging up are lowered to indicate that the debt to the red spirits will soon be met. The group's allies rub certain trees with magical fight packages, then uproot these trees, singing a song about killing called *welowe* (Rappaport 1968, p. 183). In another ritual, experts remove the supposed corruption that comes from the spirits of killed enemies and the effects of hostile *kum* sorcery that enemy experts may have placed secretly in the ceremonial ground where the *kaiko* is held. The hosts decorate themselves elaborately for the dance that goes with the pig-killing, and ritual experts apply magic fight packages to their feet to enable them to dance well and attract visiting unmarried girls. A special headdress, called the *mamp gunc*, is supposed to be worn by young men whose agnatic kin have killed enemies in the preceding fight. It is an obligation for those designated to be successors to the ritual knowledge of fight magic men to wear this decoration. At the climactic distribution of meat, recipients come forward shouting out and swinging their axes, followed by others brandishing spears

(Rappaport 1968, p. 217). This sequence is a roll-call for those who will help in the next round of fighting. The host group's men at first stay inside a ceremonial enclosure, but finally break out of it with a charge, and mingle with their guests.

After an earlier *kaiko* cycle of 1953–1954, the Tsembaga entered into fighting within three months of the *kaiko's* completion, Rappaport was told (p. 218). He was also told that in the past, peace-making ceremonies might be held instead of fighting, but he did not gain much detail about this. The model of going to war for sacred revenge was dominant, until enforced colonial pacification halted it.

The Maring example presents us with a preciously detailed account of how a structure of sacred revenge acted as the pivot of a whole ecological, cosmic, and political set of group relations. How does this compare with Ongka's brief account, which we discussed earlier?

The basic Hagen structure is the same as that for the Maring, but with two differences. First, Ongka presents the sequence as a result of choice and inclination, and he does not invoke a special category of red spirits or the Female Spirit as presiding over the imperatives of vengeance. A celebration of a powerful Female Spirit was important in Hagen cosmology, but this Spirit was specifically not tied in with warfare but with generational fertility.

Second, Ongka does not connect the payment of reparations to allies with an immediate imperative to resume waging war in order to gain revenge or satisfy dead spirits of his own group. Doubtless, fighting did start up, and a group would not engage in it without first paying their allies for their losses, but the cycle to start up warfare again was not ritually mandated. The existence of leaders who pursued *moka* exchanges also provided an alternative pathway. Thus, we hypothesize that the development of exchange- based leadership marks the growth of an elementary structure based on revenge into a complex structure based on the expansive marshalling of wealth items.

In other respects, Ongka's account is close to the Maring case. In deciding to finish a period of fighting, the roads of warfare were closed up. Years were spent in rearing pigs. When the pigs became too numerous and troublesome to care for, there would be a decision to hold the feast for the allies, just as Rappaport also mentions for the Maring (Rappaport 1968, p. 158), stressing that the bulk of the labor fell on women, as was also true for Hagen. At the end of the sequence, however, re-entry into warfare was a choice rather than an obligation, although individuals might pursue revenge by clandestine attacks or via sorcery. The opening out of relationships into exchange was perhaps correlated with the availability of valuables such as pearl shells coming from the south, a process that was greatly accelerated by colonial influences from the 1930s onward, when open warfare was halted and shells were brought in by plane as trading items and as payments for laboring work.

Variant Ontologies: Extensions of the Model of Sacred Revenge

In this section we examine further cases of revenge practices from ethnographies, keeping in mind two questions. The first is, was revenge in the societies we discuss always sacred in the sense we have chosen here, i.e., that it was sanctioned and in fact required by ancestral or other spirits? The second is, what shifts and variations can be discerned in the patterns built on the model of sacred revenge?

We begin with the well-known work of Roger Keesing on the Kwaio of Malaita in the Solomon Islands. In his book *Custom and Confrontation* (Keesing 1992, based on more than thirty years of intermittent field experience with the Kwaio people), Keesing commented on the remarkable way in which this small population of a few thousand people, living up in the mountains, had maintained their autonomy and some of their own practices despite a turbulent history of changes brought by their colonial experiences with the British Administration and with Christian missionaries: a history including the killings of outsiders as a part of the Kwaio's drive for autonomy (Keesing, op. cit. p. 4). Keesing's main concern in this book is with the Kwaio's resistance to outside control, and he extends this to the anti-colonial killings of the 1920s. He writes (p. 6) of a "logic of opposition and inversion" in Kwaio discourse. By this he means that the Kwaio have often appropriated the symbols of colonial domination and reinterpreted them in their own terms, while taking on board some of the same conceptualizations they sought otherwise to oppose. One custom they held to fiercely was their ethic of revenge.

The Kwaio, as Keesing presented them, were extraordinarily conscious of egregious ancestral figures in their genealogies and "epic chants" (Keesing, op. cit., p. 17). Keesing knew one man, Maena'adi, who held onto much knowledge derived from the past (rather as the leader Ongka did among the Melpa-speakers of Mount Hagen), a knowledge that was preserved in the chants sung to the accompaniment of pan pipes played at mortuary feasts for notable leaders, with their ghosts (*adalo*) held to be among those listening. Keesing reports on a feast he attended for the death of Tagi'au, the father of Maena'adi, who had been involved in early reprisals against the British colonial Administration and the killing of District Officer Bell in 1927. The killing of Bell and other events of violence in the epic chants were described as *mae*, and the epics were *ai'imae*. Keesing refers to the chants as describing funeral feasts, "blood feuds and punitive ancestors" (p. 17). Magical spells depended on the recitation of long genealogies, so rituals of power constantly linked the living to the dead, and the unseen presence of ancestral ghosts was a taken-for-granted part of life, substantiated by omens, dreams, and divination practices.

Informants told Keesing that some groups specialized in the production of crops and others in aggressive warriorhood, marked by the influence wielded by *lamo*, who were leaders in combat, and were also "executioners and bounty hunters" (p. 30).

Executioners? Keesing was very aware of the dangers of ethnocentric terms in the English language when dealing with Kwaio practices. However, the term "executioner" refers to what we would call "sacred revenge," sacred redressive action to put matters right. Somewhat surprisingly, Keesing writes that a blood feud would "prototypically" (p. 30) begin with a case where the rigid rules of separation between the sexes were broken by a "seduction" (not "rape," n.b.) of an unmarried girl (ibid.). The girl was then supposed to break the taboo of spatial separation between women and men by going into the men's house in her settlement and confessing the event. She would then be strangled by her brothers or other close relatives. Following this act of immediate and severe reprisal, a reward ("blood bounty," ibid.) would be set by the relatives for someone to kill the "seducer" or a close kinsman of his. (One must wonder here if a girl would in fact always report such a sexual encounter if the imminent upshot was to be her own violent death at the hands of her brothers.)

Keesing continues. The killing of the seducer might end things, or he might take refuge with his maternal kin who would be bound to protect him and would in turn be at risk of being attacked and killed. Those seeking revenge and those targeted, as entire groups, might then take refuge in defensive forts. One killing would then lead to another, and so on in a chain, as recounted in the *ai'mae* epics; some deaths are narrated as brought about by sorcery, others as physical killings accompanied by acts of deliberate insult via eating the body of a killed enemy (a physical enactment of what was a symbolic theme in Hagen stories of revenge).

It is evident that this mise en scène is quite different from the Hagen /
Maring model. First, it starts from a sexual violation, not an encounter in
fighting. Second, the violation is referred to an avenger who can receive
a reward for the killing. Who, then, could act in this way? If it could be
anyone bold enough to do it, this might widen the sphere of conflict.
In Hagen, a person might be secretly hired in this way in a case where it
would be hard for the aggrieved persons to do the killing themselves.
The process was called *el klöngi*, and the one who undertook to do the killing
by sorcery in this way was said to "take the cordyline" (*köyö titim*).
(The cordyline is a powerful symbol equated with the life force of
a person.) But this was not the prototypical case of sacred revenge. Also,
there was no actual cannibalism in Hagen practices. A shared feature is that in
all ethnographic cases, the revenge takers call on the support of their ancestral
kin to help them succeed, making the act of taking revenge axiomatically
sacred.

Another striking difference, however, flows from Keesing's report that
women were often targeted in revenge actions. In one case, which is hard to
make sense of, the "bounty hunter" shot with his rifle (an introduced weapon)
the deserted wife of a man who had eloped with the wife's sister and had
escaped punitive killing through being protected by his own kin. How this
could result in the claiming of a bounty is unclear. Keesing makes it clear,
however, that leaders (*lamo*) made a practice of taking on bounty killings and
claiming the rewards of wealth for these. This sets Kwaio leaders quite apart
from Hagen "big-men" and their winning of prestige through the *moka*
exchanges. One informant made it clear to Keesing that the whole bounty
system was open to false accusations and manipulation. *Lamo* acted as hired
killers, expanding and distorting an elementary structure of revenge. And the
genesis of revenge lay in rigid sexual rules and the violent male response to
their infractions rather than in inter-group warfare. It was therefore a system

with unstable inter-group potentialities, not geared to a fixed set of political relations among groups.

Let us look now at another ethnographic example where a version of sacred revenge operates very strongly but again in a way that topologically stretches relationships in a way different from the Hagen / Maring model. This is the case of the Gebusi people, who belong to a Lowlands region south of the Papua New Guinea Highlands (Knauft 1985). The Gebusi were a relatively small population of a few hundred (450 in 1980) living in a rain-forest environment in longhouses that contained mixed sets of kin and affines. At the time of Knauft's first ethnography, their economy was based on sago cultivation and other vegetable crops, without a large capacity for expansion. Around the longhouse there would be hamlets and isolated houses close to gardens. Epidemic diseases caused further depopulation, and the Gebusi were inclined to attribute deaths to the action of sorcerers, requiring divination to establish the sorcerer's identity and actions of physical violence to avenge the putative sorcery killing. This kind of retributive action can well be called "sacred revenge."

The Gebusi, as a small and scattered population, were subject to physical raids by the more numerous neighboring Bedamini people. Retaliation against these raids was not a viable option. Instead retribution would be taken only within the spirit world of sorcery and divinatory seances to identify sorcerers.

Knauft aptly named his book *Good Company and Violence* (Knauft 1985). Within the community as he studied it first in 1980 onward, there was a very pronounced ethos of "good company," and a reluctance to pursue accusations or suspicions of sorcery (Knauft op. cit., p. 112). Close kin, Knauft writes, would berate each other openly for allowing the death to happen, and skirt around the question of who had made the sorcery to cause the death. The close kin also had to give food generously at the funeral feast to whoever came as visitors, regardless of whether a guest was also suspected of being a sorcerer. In the end, however, anger over the death had to be assuaged, and "the sorcerer must be killed" (p. 112). Knauft refers to such killings as executions (p. 114), the term also used by Keesing for Kwaio hired revenge killings.

The Gebusi had already been subject to colonial control by the Australian Administration when Knauft began his work there, so figures that he impressively provides for numbers of deaths attributed to physical killings ("homicides" is his term) vary according to whether they related to pre- or post-contact times. In pre-contact times, adult females were reported to be killed at a rate 20 percent less than adult men. In post-contact times, with an administrative ban on homicides, "the homicide rate for women has become more than twice that of men" (p. 117). This was because killing a woman, especially if she was a widow and without protectors, was easier to carry out and easier to conceal from the authorities than killing a man. Still, both men and women could be targets.

Knauft goes on to note that 60.7 percent of killings were said to be killings of people accused of sorcery. (What the other 39.3 percent of killings were said to be about would be another topic.) Mostly these killings did not result in a chain of retaliatory killings. (Note the remarkable difference here from the the Kwaio case, where an indefinite chain of killings might take place.) This shows, Knauft argues, that these killings of persons divined to have killed a victim by sorcery were, in a sense, executions accepted as legitimate. Such executions, then, were carried out deliberately by raids against their immediate target. In other words, they were not a part of warfare: we are not dealing with war as a category here, hence Knauft's choice of the term "homicide." Pitched battles were rare in Knauft's extensive sample of cases and greatly inhibited by cross-cutting ties of kinship and marriage. In addition, the Gebusi said that young, never-married females could not be sorcerers, thus exempting them from being targets of revenge killings (and, one might add, ensuring some viability for creating marriages by "sister exchange" and ensuring reproduction of the population).

Raids to kill a person accused of killing someone by sorcery did not usually result in reprisals against the raiders, partly because of a tendency to acquiesce in the results of divination and partly because the assembled attacking group was stronger than the defendants, or because kin of the accused simply fled rather than resisting the attack (p. 126). In only a few cases a suspected sorcerer was thought to have been motivated by revenge (ibid.). We can surmise that if it were granted that a putative sorcerer had acted out of a legitimate desire for revenge, it would be hard, if not impossible, to justify killing them, so this example shows the ways in which the ideology has to work.

In some instances a senior person thought to have killed others by sorcery might be magically attacked by a relative of the supposed victim asking clan ancestors to find and kill the culprits. If the accused fell sick and then died, this was taken as proof that the ancestors had undertaken to act in accordance with the magical entreaty. In one case Knauft mentions that a man entreated for such a death against his own widowed sister after she was accused of sorcery on several occasions. (Perhaps he did so to avoid being killed himself instead of her?) Agnates of a person who died of sickness were the ones who usually initiated accusations of sorcery and carried out killings as retaliations. Sometimes they would have an unrelated person carry out the retaliations for a contract (cf. Kwaio bounty killings and the Hagen *el klöngi* described earlier). This practice went into decline after government control because such killings were forbidden and therefore became risky.

Knauft's account further explores the different categories of sorcery. For example, *ogowili* is assault sorcery and said to be carried out only by men and used against a single victim whom they found alone on a forest path. When people are with someone, they are thought to repel the *ogowili*. If an *ogowili* is suspected, their kinsfolk, too, are thought to protect them (p. 134). The *ogowili* may be suspected of killing and eating his victim, and if so he may be attacked, killed, and eaten in retaliation, in what Knauft rightly called "exact reciprocity" (p. 134). Another type of sorcery was *bogay*, package sorcery, in which a parcel of magical substance was placed so as to attack and kill someone. The putative attacker was thought to be someone like the victim, and in one case, after being identified and captured, he was dressed in initiation costume to signal a symbolic equivalence to the age of his victim before being killed and eaten (p. 135). Parcel sorcery is the category that was most often identified as the cause of a death and most often led to a killing in reprisal. The parcel sorcerer was not seen as a dangerous warrior, as the *ogowili* was. Moreover, parcel sorcery accusations most often occurred between members of the same community. (Here, too, there is a difference with Hagen, where sorcery suspicions were usually centered on persons outside of the community unless they fell on an in-married wife from an enemy group.) Such accusations among the Gebusi would at first be presented lightly and without immediate action, but later the accused person would nevertheless be killed, replacing "good company" with condign violence.

The question arises, how were suspicions arrived at and tested? Divination was resorted to, exercised by a spirit medium who was thought to enlist the help of spirits. Divination might also involve a test in which the accused had to provide a stick of sago for cooking, and if it was not properly baked, they were held to be guilty. Besides, such a system of attribution does not require that the accused person has a grievance. Rather the sorcerer's action is held to be simply malicious. Sacred revenge, again then, is thus easily justified without fear of rebuttal. If any justification or reason for a putative sorcerer's actions was offered, it had to do with anger over a failure to meet standards of reciprocity in marriage arrangements that were prototypically supposed to be by sister exchange (p. 146). There is here a vestige of a counter-ideology that says the sorcerer himself is acting in a "payback" capacity. And in some cases, a clan that had not kept to its exchange obligations might be afflicted with sorcery accusations and killed off (p. 147). Knauft notes further (p. 152) that "no cases of sorcery attribution" happened between clans allied by an existing sister exchange. In other words, where the marital arrangements were in balance, accusations of sorcery would not be made. "Sacred revenge" therefore was justified by both the divinatory work of spirit mediums and by acts of punishing failures to keep to the "rules" of reciprocity in marriage and reproduction in this small-scale, atomistic, and egalitarian society. We have found sacred revenge, then, as a central theme among the Gebusi, but worked out in a very different way from other cases we have looked at.

In all cases, however, and in a broader sense, revenge is action taken to balance a ledger of strength in both reproduction and exchange. Knauft summarizes this part of his exposition by stating that "the existence of marital imbalance is a crucial magnet for sorcery attribution" (p. 156). Sacred revenge is here, then, calqued onto a notional system of sister exchange marriage, and the alliance relationships that flow from this practice. The effects of marriages of particular types become intertwined with sorcery attribution over time, for example in cases where men marry classificatory sisters from brother clans to their own. Sorcery accusations may arise between them, and this type of marriage is supposed to be forbidden. The sister-exchange preference itself produces tensions, because within a small patriline a young man may not have an available sister to be part of such an exchange. Notably, if there is no possibility of a sister exchange, some goods may be given to obtain a wife. But Knauft denies that this is to be seen as any kind of bridewealth, and he adds emphatically that "Gebusi have no tradition of making compensation payments in any dimension of social life" (p. 170). This observation reveals a fundamental distinction between a Gebusi-type elementary marriage system and a Hagen-type complex system of bridewealth and exchange.

Affines, whether as a result of sister exchange or not, are enjoined to be friendly, but only as long as the woman who links them remains alive (p. 172). If the woman dies, sorcery accusations can arise, especially if the marriage was not reciprocal, that is, not based on sister exchange. Romantic marriages play further into this complex. Gebusi actually favor marriages based on mutual sexual attraction, and this can violate a sister exchange arrangement, thus leading into latent conflict over time (p. 173). As Knauft notes, this does not mean that we should attribute all problems to this structural fault in the system, but in conjunction with a lack of a developed model of exchanges of wealth as are found in Hagen and elsewhere, the pathway is left open for conflicts over reciprocity. Knauft also shows the further complications that arose between Gebusi and neighboring groups. The Bedamini were strong and could exact compensation in pigs from Gebusi over supposed sorcery deaths. The Oybae were weak and suffered predations by Gebusi who attempted to capture women from them for marriage (p. 229). When unreciprocated marriages occurred, it was assumed that the disgruntled side might engage in retaliatory sorcery over time.

Finally, here, spirit mediums held a privileged place in the cosmic scheme of things. They were less likely to be accused of sorcery than others, and their deaths were more likely to be avenged (p. 236). Spirit mediums played a pivotal part in politics here in the same way as "big-men" leaders did, and do, in Hagen. Their wealth lay not in pigs and shells but in their rhetorical powers to act as ventriloquists of the spirits.

Structures in History: The Enga

At an earlier point in our discussion we affirmed the point that in order for revenge to be transformed into wealth exchange there must first be an idea of commensurability between humans and wealth goods. We have seen that this concept was not present among the Gebusi, other than in sporadic forced exchanges with their more powerful neighbors, the Bedamini. Another case from the fringes of the Highlands, on the Daribi people, intensively expounded by Roy Wagner, supplies an instance where the principle of equivalence between persons and wealth is clearly operative and worked into gifts to maternal kin and for bridewealth exchanges, but competitive exchanges of wealth did not develop (Wagner 1981). History is always intersecting with culture, and vice versa, so that a cultural principle or value may be at work, but without the material conditions that would lead it to develop in further ways.

We turn now to an ethnographic case where a great deal of research has been carried out, and historical processes have been extracted from work on oral histories. This is the complex case of the Enga, a large congeries of people speaking various dialects and living to the west of the Hagen area. The Enga are famous in the ethnographic record for their highly developed system of enchained exchanges of wealth in pigs and cooked pork that link together large numbers of local groups. This system is called the *Tee* (or *Te*). A similar set of developments, although not on the same scale, was observed in fieldwork in the Dei Council area of Hagen in the 1960s (Strathern 1971, reprinted with new Introduction 2007). Discussion of the evolution of regional integrative exchanges of this kind is of great interest. Our purpose here, however, is to find within the Enga system a kernel of how the *Tee* may have emerged from forms of compensation such as war reparations, or at least how war reparations, organized on a clan basis and paid to both allies and former enemies, run as a common denominator along with *Tee* exchanges.

In the exposition of Wiessner and Tumu 1998, Enga war reparations were *not* based in "the substitution of wealth for human life" (1998, p. 146). A death by killing still had in principle to be paid for by an act of revenge (= "sacred revenge"). What reparations could do was to renew positive ties between people, ties on which social life in general depended. To enemies, compensation payments meant that social boundaries would not have to be breached by further fighting. So, reparations and compensation were to keep the peace, and give scope for peaceful leadership. The question arises, how then was payback killing to be fitted into such a scheme of things? Perhaps the answer is that the payback was thought to be carried out by sorcery, an unverified and hidden act, so that it would not cause a regeneration of fighting. Growing population density seems to have been the factor driving these processes. Reparations in fact at first took the form of land and foods, only later incorporating valuable pearl shells when these began arriving in trade routes from Tambul and the south (p. 248). With enemies, the previous practice had been to dislodge them and drive them away. As the land filled up, such dispersals became less possible and clan boundaries had to be more settled. Payments of compensation to enemies depended on marriage ties or on extended "brother" relations. The structure here is like Hagen "minor enemy" relations. As in Hagen also, initiatory gifts were made to solicit a larger reparation payment (p. 251). With the extension of payments to (some) enemies, powers of mediation and influence by leaders became of greater importance. Big-manship and extensions of reparations went together, exactly as took place in Hagen in the 1960s.

Further categories detailed by Wiessner and Tumu (1998, p. 256) also closely parallel Hagen procedures, including initiatory gifts and final payment (*akali buingi*, in Melpa *wuö metemen*) that were expected to exceed the initiatory gifts received. This is the ground plan for *moka* exchange in Hagen too. As in Hagen, also, all such processes were put at risk if anyone in a victim's clan felt left out or was aggrieved. Here we find confirmation that all such issues were contingencies, and we may therefore revisit the argument made by Wiessner and Tumu, that reparation payments do not mean that there is a symbolic equivalence between wealth forms and human life. Perhaps we can say that at

Elements in Religion and Violence

a cultural level there is in fact a general sense of commensurability between a life and wealth goods, but this does not mean there is an exact equivalence in social practice. In negotiations over reparations, a victim's group may insist that no payment can be enough for a life lost, while at the same time agreeing that they will accept a payment to make themselves feel better and to resume social relations of alliance and exchange, in accordance with the explanations given to Wiessner and Tumu. Indeed, we can go further and say that the same pragmatic contingency applies also in Hagen. Thus, the Hagen and Enga ethnography can be brought into alignment. That this is plausible is supported by the additional observations already made above that reparations including "extra" pigs given to a victim's clan (Wiessner and Tumu, p. 258), were described as "profit" pigs by their informant Kyakas. Such an idea also forms the ground plan in Hagen for the emergence of *moka* exchange practices. A *moka* gift must exceed a gift received before, in the first place an initiatory gift soliciting the *moka*. As Wiessner and Tumu observe, time was also a factor. It took time to raise pigs for a reparation and leaders worked hard to ensure that everyone took part and there were no complaints on either side. Speeches made by leaders were important in both promising that gifts would be made and in keeping recipients waiting until everything was ready (see, for comparison, speeches made by Ongka-Kaepa in the film *Ongka's Big Moka*, Granada Television 1974).

As we have also stressed in our book *Peace-Making and the Imagination* (Strathern and Stewart 2011), the whole complex process of peace-making is to be understood as a form of ritualization of relationships in which hostility is replaced by amity or formal friendship, and the replacement occurs gradually and in stages. For the Enga, Wiessner and Tumu note that as a part of peace-making between groups that had few strong ties, a *kauma pingi*, or formal dance, could be held at which marriages between the groups would be arranged (p. 262). Exchange would thus replace hostility as a form of "boundary maintenance," Wiessner and Tumu remark, although these would be very different sorts of sociality, since exchanges lead to the modification of boundaries as well as, in a different way, their maintenance through the avoidance of armed conflict and displacement of one side by the other. Growing population density made all this more compelling, as Wiessner and Tumu several times note (e.g., p. 264). In an extraordinary further development out of war reparations, Wiessner and Tumu show that in some parts of the Enga area, elaborate war tournaments were held that were expected to result in reparation payments and exchanges between those involved. These tournaments may be described as "epideictic displays" in the terms Roy Rappaport used in his discussion of the Maring (Rappaport 1968): that is, ritual displays of numbers and strength designed to achieve parity with or dominance over others. They were also arenas in which specialist leaders, called *watenge*, could joust with each other by oratory and mobilization of followers. The ritualized aspect of all this is shown by the fact that the lives of the *watenge* were to be respected. They were not to be killed (Wiessner and Tumu 1998, p. 269). This is a vital point for our overall theme. Why this particular ritual restraint on killing? Because, we suggest, if the *watenge* were killed, serious sacred revenge would have to be brought into play, and the whole "game" of the tournaments seems to have been to bypass revenge and move directly into exchange. The tournaments represent the transcendence of revenge by exchange, comparable to the negotiated obviation of revenge in the Hagen *moka* system, where the exchanges themselves became the focus of competition for prestige.

Envoi: Gifts and Violence

In Hagen sacred revenge killings were transmuted gradually and contingently into competitive exchanges of wealth. Agonistic exchange that raised the intensity of such competition to a point beyond sustainability would represent a level of cultural involution that would ultimately defeat the initial aim of exchanges of wealth, that is, to create peaceful political relations between groups and individuals in networks. However, in Hagen this situation did not arise because groups never took their competitions to that point and because there was always a limit on the amounts of wealth that either side could raise. Moreover, the process in Hagen, as everywhere else, was greatly inflected by the imposition of colonial pacification, followed by the turbulence of rebounding violence in the context of rapid changes, movements of persons, uneven economic development, and conflict between stakeholders in the post-colonial parliamentary system of elections. Renewed killings, whether in fighting or in road accidents, led to a need to make compensation payments in order to avoid violence. Here we come to the crux of the matter. The purpose of "the gift" in this case is propitiatory, to avoid a retributive action in response to an act of violence. The gift is reactive, a response to another situation provoked by violence. Moreover, such a gift is also a sacrifice, because it typically involves killing a pig or pigs as an offering. This circumstance is clear in all the examples from the Papua New Guinea Highlands. How well does this sit with the famous and foundational work of Marcel Mauss on "The Gift," invariably cited in introductory courses in anthropology and influential at a theoretical level in terms of the proposition that objects as gifts are to be seen in Pacific Island contexts as having agency? "The thing given is not inert. It is alive and often personified" (Mauss 1969 [original in French 1925]). This observation was widely taken up and proved to be an inspiration to many an ethnographic analysis in a culturalist vein on Pacific peoples.

Mauss drew on materials from a range of Polynesian societies for his investigation, but it is notable that his own specific inspiration came from Maori materials, and via a text collected from a Maori informant of the ethnographer Elsdon Best, Tamati Ranaipiri. He explained the linked meanings of *taonga* and *hau*. *Taonga* is any valuable possession that can be given between people.

If a person gives such a *taonga* to someone, the recipient may give it in turn to another person. That recipient, after a while, will find another *taonga* and give this to the one he received the original *taonga* from. Now this latest *taonga* in the chain is the *hau* ("spirit") of the *taonga* that was first given. If a person in the chain declined to pass on a *taonga* they had received back to the originator of the chain, that person might become ill or actually die. The *hau* wants the circulating *taonga* to return to the home of the original giver.

This is a very explicit account of the workings of chains of reciprocity in a society where gifts of valuable items are important in sustaining social relations. It is interesting that the *hau* carries with it a sanction, since anyone who does not comply with its "wishes" or "desire" feels that they may fall sick. Also, the initial act of making returns for receipt of a *taonga* is categorized as *utu*, a Maori term that Mauss notes means also "satisfaction in blood vengeance" (Mauss, op. cit., note 27, p. 86). *Utu* can therefore signify something given as compensation for a killing, and if an *utu* were not given it would certainly provoke an act of vengeance, perhaps by sorcery if not by open physical violence. In an earlier discussion (chapter 9 of *Exchange and Sacrifice*, Stewart and Strathern 2008) we have suggested that the "spirit of the gift" is the same as the spirit of the *moka* as an institution based on the satisfaction of interlocking debts, with a basic triadic rather than a dyadic structure. Now, for both the *moka* and the *hau/taonga* complex, it is evident that the potential sanction on failure or refusal to respect the flow of valuables is the exercise of retaliatory violence (or "sacred revenge"). In the case of *hau* the capacity for retaliation is thought to reside in the *hau* itself, since if someone holds onto a *taonga*, its *hau* "avenges the theft, controls the thief, bewitches him and leads him to death or constrains him to restore the object" (Mauss, op. cit., p. 86, note 29).

Exactly how the circulation of *taonga* intersected in the past with feuding and fights between kin groups (*hapu*) and their chiefs would be interesting to explore further. What is clear from Maori accounts and also accounts of lethal disputes in the origin places from which the Maori came to Aotearoa/ New Zealand such as Rarotonga in the Cook Islands is that Maori chiefs were very concerned about the preservation of their honor or *mana* (power), were insistent on the maintenance of *tapu* rules regulating rights over property and persons, and were ready to engage in violent action to support these concerns. Arriving on long voyages from a distant region of small islands into new territories larger than they could have had available where they came from, they probably expanded their population and were engaged in warfare with one another to do so. They built *pa*, fortified stockades, to withstand massed attacks, ambushes, raids, and sieges. One such *pa* in the South Island of Aotearoa was established in the Purakaunui area near what later became the city of Dunedin, founded subsequently by Scottish settlers. The *pa* was built on a small peninsula that juts out into the turbulent sea on the coast and has been dubbed "Goat Island." The *pa* was called Mapoutahi *pa*. The spot is now a favorite for visitors to the beach, but at the entry to it there is a notice advising people of the conflicts that took place there and to respect the spirits of Maori who were killed there in an internecine struggle centered on pride and revenge.

Oral narratives recount how, some seven generations ago, there was a chief called Taonga (his very name means "precious," it may be noted, because it is the same term as that used for valuable wealth items used in gift-giving, as we have discussed above). He lived at Timaru, on the coast a long way north of Purakaunui. One day he decided to visit a cousin of his, Te Wera, of the Ngatimamoe clan, who lived in a large *pa* at Karitane, quite close to Purakaunui (northwards up the coastline). Te Wera and Taonga then set out to visit another kinsman, Kapo, at Mapoutahi. Te Wera was known as a hot-tempered man who had killed his own wife, a high-ranking woman of the Kai Tahu tribe (*iwi*) in the South Island. (The narrative does not explain what repercussions there were from this killing, but it does record the results of what happened next.) The two chiefs fell into an altercation. (Over what? These narratives often offer apparently small reasons for massive conflicts, the explanation of which has to do with competitive senses of *mana*.) Te Wera killed Taonga's son in the quarrel, and Taonga vowed to take revenge. These two chiefs were cousins, but the killing of Taonga's son was an act that required an act of revenge; it was too heinous for it to be settled by an *utu* payment. Te Wera was a host, and in killing a high- ranking guest, he was committing kohuru, "murder."

Taonga went back to Timaru and gathered his fighters, then returned and laid siege to the Karitane *pa*. Unable to take this *pa*, Taonga returned the following winter and besieged the Mapoutahi *pa*, belonging to Kapo, the ally of Te Wera. Under cover of a severe snow storm, Taonga led his men into the *pa*, which was undefended at the time, and once inside they killed 250 people, while a few escaped by jumping off the rock face into the ocean (*The New Zealand Railways Magazine*, vol. 13, Issue 1, January 1, 1939, pp. 43–44).

If all this was considered a justifiable act of revenge against Te Wera for the killing of Taonga's son, we can only speculate again how any kind of peace settlement between the chiefs could have been worked out. The "sacred revenge" in question was not even enacted against Te Wera himself but against an ally of his. Would Te Wera have to pay reparations to his allies for this terrible loss? How could he possibly do so? Feuds over killings could continue for very long periods of time. Could a *taonga* be so valuable that it could atone for many deaths? The study of questions like this would require much more detailed information. Here, we simply raise these questions out of an interest in how *taonga* might be employed to settle conflicts, as shells and pigs were in the Papua New Guinea Highlands. But how do you transcend the massacre of 250 people?

A striking film, *The Dead Lands*, produced in 2014, starts out with a comparable event, the massacre of the kinsfolk of a young son of a Maori chief, carried out by a neighboring group. As the sole remaining male descendant, the youth bears the responsibility of claiming back the *mana* of his *hapu* by wreaking vengeance on the murderers of his father and the father's kin. How can he possibly do this against all odds? There is an area of ill omen, where an ancient group was murdered and destroyed, called The Dead Lands, where the youth has to make a kind of fateful journey and encounters and gains the support of an entity, half-spirit, half-man, who is a powerful warrior. The warrior himself is the only male survivor of his own group that was massacred, hence the name The Dead Lands. The two together seek to take revenge on the young man's enemies. The redoubtable "warrior" kills many of their opponents, but in the assault on the heavily guarded *pa* of the enemies even the apparently invincible warrior is mortally wounded while trying to help the youth in a deadly individual combat. The youth, having gained entry into the stockade, must now continue on his own to fight his counterpart, a chiefly youth who thinks himself the stronger fighter and was a ruthless ringleader in the attack on the youth's kin. Helped by the spirit of the warrior, the young hero overcomes his enemy in a titanic combat. His defeated opponent offers himself to be killed, in accordance with his sense of honor and his rank. However, in a striking volte face the victorious youth declines to dispatch him, releasing him instead with a warning never to interfere with him or his people again. The opponent's *mana* is destroyed by this act of "forgiveness," or rather refusal to kill, and the feud between the two sides is conclusively brought to an end, with the humiliation of the defeated enemy. Here is another portrayal of a ritualized transcendence of sacred revenge, not by payments of wealth, but by breaking the chain of killings themselves. It was more effective to destroy the sacred power of the enemy by not killing him. Sparing the enemy, the youth shames him and effectively disbars him from re-entering the tournament of honor and dominance that fuels sacred revenge. The victor takes the persona and power of his enemy away, leaving him only the shadow of his former self.

It is another way of killing, just as in the *moka* film("Ongka's Big Moka") Ongka said he had knocked down his opponent by the size of the gifts he gave him. In the Dead Lands film the Maori hero takes away the social life of his enemy by giving him his physical life, which he will have to endure as a "failed" warrior. By transcending a physical sacred revenge, the hero inflicts a more devastating symbolic sacred revenge on his erstwhile foe. He thus also brings justice back into the world.

Broader Contexts

We have seen, following the expansion of the topic of revenge from the immediate process of killing into the wider conspectus of restoring balance in the cosmos, or order of forces in the life world, that revenge becomes sacred when it is linked to an aim of restoring a balance that is felt to be disturbed. It is worthwhile to note again that an aim of this kind is commonly found in narratives around the world. Expanded again, the theme of balance and counter-balance can be seen as applying to ecological as well as social issues. In this section, then, we take up and illustrate these points in three contexts. One is a narrative from a story called "The Witchfinder," by S. Fowler Wright, centering on struggles between noble families in England and on accusations of witchcraft. Our second context will be Homer's *Odyssey*, in which Odysseus's final revenge against the dissolute suitors attempting to court his wife Penelope after his presumed death in his wanderings after the Trojan War can be interpreted as a sacred act. Our third example will take us back to Papua New Guinea and its Highlands region, well known for its emphasis on revenge killings, but drawing on our work among the Duna people of Hela Province, and detailing people's reactions to cosmic disturbances, including the ecological effects of mining enterprises.

The "Witchfinder" story begins with a nobleman, Sir John, fleeing from a scene in which he had killed an assailant and was being pursued by four others seeking his life in retaliation. His opponents were in the service of his enemy, Sir Hugh Offley, led by Sir Hugh himself. Sir John dispenses with his horse and much of his weaponry, and hides overnight, then walks on till he comes to a ruined cottage. Hiding again, he sees two women walking along a pathway, one of striking appearance and tall, the other short, her face hidden in a bonnet. Suddenly the taller one pushes the shorter one into a disused well and walks off. Sir John emerges and tries to save the woman pushed into the well but has to break off because he hears his enemies approaching on horseback and he must hide from them. They arrive, find the woman in a bad state but alive, and pull her out of the well. Sir John goes on his way, undiscovered. He enters a cottage in search of food and water, finds there the young woman he had seen push the older one into the well, and she helps him because Sir Hugh Offley is her enemy also. Offley's party tracks them down to the cottage and demands entry, which she successfully denies them.

Sir Hugh tries to intimidate her, saying she is the child of a witch, her grandmother, who has been accused of witchcraft by an informer. The enemies nevertheless leave, while threatening to return with a search warrant. The young woman explains to Sir John that her father had once given refuge to a stranger lost in the woods, who was actually the king and had out of gratitude given her father the right to live indefinitely in the cottage and to hunt for game around it, a right that had passed to her as his heir. All the rest of the forest around belonged to Sir Hugh. She explains that in order to evict her and seize her property, Sir Hugh was having her grandmother falsely declared a witch by the authorities.

Sir Hugh arranges to have the local sheriff arrive with a warrant of arrest for the grandmother. The young woman, Margot, comments that if there is a just God, it is the person who has ordered the warrant (Sir Hugh) who ought to be afraid. This is a significant remark, indicating that the whole story is a narrative of divination to determine good and evil, and that its outcome will be an act of sacred revenge.

Margot is assured by the sheriff and by the religious authority who is with him, the Prior of Monceaux, that there is a just God and if her grandmother is innocent of witchcraft, she need not fear a trial. The Prior, however, had sent five women to be burnt at the stake as witches in the previous two years, on the basis of accusations made by an informant, so Margot is not reassured.

The story continues. Sir Hugh attempts to have Sir John arrested for the killing of his servant. Sir John, however, shows a Latin document coming from the king, indicating that he has been recently knighted and has the king's favor, and so his killing of the servant was to be considered an act of knightly self-defense. He also learns that Margot's act against the other woman was done because this was the woman who had falsely witnessed against the five women burnt as witches for pay in gold coins and had planned to sell Margot's grandmother's life for more pay. So Margot also sees her own act against the woman as an act of sacred revenge taken on the informer who had sent five women to their death with lies about them. Margot's act of pushing the woman into the well thus brought to her a feeling of payback, retribution, and a personal sense of justice done (*autrement dit*, "sacred revenge"). But neither Margot nor Sir John know if the informer had drowned or had survived or had been saved.

Margot and Hugh ride swiftly, making a difficult river crossing, to encounter the sheriff's party, which is taking her grandmother to trial. They manage to confront and halt the sheriff's group by blocking the path, and Sir John tells the Prior that Sir Hugh had raised a false charge against Margot's grandmother. The Prior replies that the witness against the grandmother is one Judith Hoad, who is said to be gifted to detect witches by marks on their bodies.

Sir John replies that perhaps the truth is that the informer is herself a witch. He says he has seen her thrown in a well without immediately drowning, so this could be a sign she is a witch herself. The Prior is given pause by this invocation of a possible divinatory truth. As it turns out later, the woman is already dead, of a fever – already a payback at the cosmic level for her false witnessing. However, none of the protagonists know this crucial fact. Sir John has recourse now to another divinatory procedure. Using an old provision of the law, he says that a champion may fight an accuser on behalf of a person accused of wrongdoing, and he demands a battle of honor with Sir Hugh on the spot before he will allow the sheriff's party to proceed.

This is a divinatory battle of a classic kind, in which the outcome will decide between good and evil, justice and injustice. Sir John is in a bad state, has no armor, and has only his poniard and his mace as weapons. The Prior realizes that the combat proposed may be a sign of God's own judgement, thus belonging to the cosmic realm. Sir John has no male supporter. As an innovation, Margot says she will take on this role. Mistakenly she fastens his mace to his wrist. He frees it again, but at the cost of breaking his poniard. Now he has only his mace.

The spectators realize that the odds are now heavily stacked against Sir John. The Prior invokes God as the judge of what will happen. The two knights charge at each other. Sir John swings his only weapon, the mace, throws it forward, and it smashes the jaw of Sir Hugh, who at once collapses and is severely wounded. The divination is complete. God has been on Sir John's side. The accusation against Margot's grandmother is thus proven false, and she is released. Sir John takes control of Sir Hugh's men. The Prior now concludes that Judith Hoad had been motivated by greed (a sin) and was an unreliable witness after all (not much help for the five women previously found guilty). Sir John tells the Prior to prepare for another ritual act, officiating at a marriage, for Sir John will now marry Margot, whose own earlier act of revenge is now fully vindicated by the greater divinatory power of the combat in which Sir John has killed Sir Hugh in an act of sacred revenge, bringing to an end Sir Hugo's dictatorial ways and restoring justice to the land.

A narrative of this kind depends on a number of cultural ideas, centering on the value of honor and the divinatory power of acts engaged in via honor. The concept of divination enables sacred revenge undertaken by humans to be aligned with the supposed judgement by an almighty God. Fowler Wright's story perfectly depicts this structure of conflict settlement (Wright 1946, pp. 7–53).

The cultural themes that underlie Fowler Wright's story are rank, honor, property rights, monarchy, and above all the importance of military prowess. In such abstract terms, it is obvious that these themes appear in comparable ways in Homer's *Odyssey*. The widest criterion of comparison has to do with how rank intersects with the wider cosmos. Success depends on the favor of the gods, or God, and the gods are seen as ultimately on the side of justice. A hero is a hero not simply because he has rank or can fight, but because he ultimately fights for what is right. This is the clear message of the "Witchfinder" story. In the *Odyssey*, the message is essentially the same, but is complicated in two ways. First, the gods are themselves pursuing their own individual concerns and taking sides in human affairs. Their presence, also, is overt and declared rather than immanent and inferred. Conflicts among the gods are partially resolved by the fact that Zeus is the supreme male god, and Pallas Athene, his daughter said to be sprung from his head, gathers some of the power of Zeus into herself, a point that is important in Homer's narrative. Athene supports Odysseus in his ultimate battle with the infamous and unbridled suitors of his faithful wife Penelope.

The gods appear generally as prime movers of action throughout the *Odyssey*. The poet invokes his Muse, asking her to start the story. He refers to the story that all of Odysseus's companions died at sea because they arrogantly stole and consumed the cattle of the sun god, Helios, not by any mistake, but by a deliberate decision, excusing themselves by saying that later they would make a sacrifice to the god. Odysseus alone is spared, and he is finally assisted by Athene and Zeus to return to his home, Ithaca, and at last enact revenge (*nemesis*) on the arrogance (*hubris*) of the suitors who have besieged his place with intent to marry Penelope, his wife, and succeed to his wealth and power.

Odysseus wanders long, until he eventually lands in Ithaca and proceeds in disguise to his place. Intent on his plan to take revenge on the suitors but staying meanwhile in the disguise of a humble wandering beggar, Odysseus inserts himself into the company of the suitors for his wife Penelope, who is gradually persuaded that it is really he who has returned and resolves to help him. On the plane of the deities, Athene, the goddess who has supported Odysseus all along, comes to him and assures him of victory against the suitors who have invaded his home and are eating up his stock animals. She strengthens his resolve. Then she puts him to sleep. Early next morning, the god Zeus, father of Athene, sends out a thunderbolt, and a handmaid at work in the palace grinding grain hails it as an omen that the suitors are about to be punished. Servants meanwhile bring in animals to be killed for the daily feast. The suitors at the same time are plotting to kill Telemachus, Odysseus's son. He, however, acts coolly and bravely in their faces. One suitor, Ctesippus, throws an ox hoof at Odysseus's head, enraging him. Odysseus is still in disguise and does not reveal his identity yet, and he appears to accept the jibe that he is just a dirty homeless wanderer.

Next day, Odysseus startles the company of suitors by successfully stringing his own great bow, left in his palace (another divinatory act). The suitors have attempted in vain to bend it and string it. They are taken aback. Odysseus then reveals himself to his servants by showing them a wound from a boar's tusk incurred years before on a hunt on Mount Parnassus. Odysseus grasps his bow and begins to shoot the suitors, one after the other, beginning with their leader, Antinous. The suitors try to buy him off, with no success. Athene then fiercely urges Odysseus on, and tests his fighting power. Athene also turns aside the spears cast at Odysseus and his helpers. Then, in return, Odysseus launches his weapons and each one meets its mark. A few are spared, at the intercession of Telemachus. Those spared crouched at the altar of Zeus in the courtyard, as suppliants for mercy. The female servants who had lain with the suitors were all killed, while Odysseus's old nurse, who had recognized him and roused those who had been faithful to the house, is restored to a position of favor. Odysseus is reunited with Penelope, and the next morning Athene sends him out to meet any fresh challenges from the slain suitors' kin groups. Sacred revenge has been achieved (Homer, *Odyssey*, Books 20–22).

The Duna example takes us into the arena of ecology, the same general context that occupied Roy Rappaport in his study of ritual cycles among the Maring people (Rappaport 1968). In our Duna example, the ecological concerns of the people themselves were overt and manifest (on the Duna see Stewart and Strathern 2002a; Strathern and Stewart 2004b). From the viewpoint of the Duna, aspects of their life-world were looked after by categories of environmental spirits. If given proper respect, these spirits would benefit the human population. A major ritual complex of actions among the Duna was called *rindi kiniya*, "repairing the ground." The earth was seen as having a tendency to lose its fertility over a number of generations, and rituals involving the sacrifice of pigs were thought to be necessary to halt this process and revive fertility. The effects of a huge gold mine in Porgera within Enga Province, connected by rivers on the edges of the Duna area, were seen in the late 1990s by the Duna people with whom we worked as deleterious to the environment around the Strickland River. Tailings from the mine reached the Strickland and were turning the water red, harming the fish in it and in particular displeasing a Female Spirit whose domain was the river water, so that she was said to have left the Duna area looking for some other living space. The mining company, while admitting no fault, agreed to pay compensation to the local groups for any loss of riparian and fishing activities.

Another company, Barrick Gold, then attempted to drill for oil in a site near the Strickland River, beyond the ordinary limits of Duna occupation but within a domain to which they had some affiliations (Stewart and Stathern 2002a). The company was unable to break through a hard rock layer over the oil deposits, and the Duna developed a narrative (which we collected in the area while the events were happening) that the drilling point had threatened a great earth giant spread over Papua New Guinea, aiming at the giant's heart. The giant, a version of a traditional category known as *tindi auwene* ("grandfather of the earth"), had prevailed upon a youth, who had found his way down to where the giant lay in the earth, to knock aside the drill and so save his life. Female Spirits were involved in helping the youth make this underground visit, it was said, and the story spread widely (Stewart and Strathern 2002a). At the time of this happening, the Duna were very concerned that extracting the oil from the earth would dry up and exhaust the fertility of the land, disrupting the cycles of its renewal. The oil was spoken of by some leaders as the repository for the vital "grease" of the ancestors who had been buried in the ground and whose body substances had turned into the oil. Removing this "grease," it was said, would have the result of drying up the land and making the indigenous rituals to repair it ineffective.

Thus, the balance of elements in the cosmos would be destroyed. The narrative about the Tindi Auwene developed as an attempt to show that the earth had, in a sense, resisted the mining exploration in order to return itself to a cosmic balance. The act of the youth in knocking aside and breaking the drill point can therefore be seen as a version of sacred revenge carried out on behalf of the environment.

In another area, Aluni, among the Duna, where we also worked, the leaders had to exercise creativity in dealing with the putative concomitants of a large forest fire that had destroyed much of their forest in the vicinity of their settlements. The fire had inadvertently been started by youths of one group who were out hunting and had left embers of a campfire behind. Large areas of forest were burnt, destroying vegetation and habitats for game animals and birds, and more significantly harming the resting places in rock shelters of spirits of the dead whose bones were sequestered there in secondary burials. The forest is also thought of as looked after by the same Female Spirit (Payame Ima) who cares for living things in and around the Strickland River. In response to this disturbance of their cosmos, the Duna leaders of Aluni developed a remarkable stabilizing ritual, staged in a remote forest clearing, consisting of a mass sacrifice of pigs to ancestors and the forest deities, marked by traditional invocations to the land by older leaders and Christian prayers by younger men, all acting in concert to re-set the cosmos. The ritual was a new version of the *rindi kiniya* (earth repairing) complex from the past. It was carried out to forestall a kind of sacred revenge on the part of the spirits by placating them and offering an apology and a sacrifice of valuable pigs. Sacred revenge was transmuted into a positive ritual of stewardship of the environment, which also creatively combined the old and new forms of ritual practice, the Christian and the pagan, in a single ritual process.

Some Ending Thoughts

In our pursuit of the topic of sacred revenge we have shown how it applies as an elementary structural model in basic contexts of conflict among a number of peoples in Oceania and elsewhere. In a broader sense we can discern the expansion of this model in a wider theme of rebalancing the cosmos and propitiating the powers of the cosmos when human actions have violated propriety or criteria of justice, or else have damaged the spirits of the environment. Such a perceived need for rebalancing the cosmos and deflecting its disturbed actions is found further in the rapidly developing contemporary arena of climate change, with shoreline erosion, cyclones and typhoons, floods, volcanic eruptions, and forest fires, and the interpretations of these processes in different parts of Oceania and beyond, for example among the indigenous Austronesian speakers of Taiwan. Most recently, deep concerns have emerged in Papua New Guinea where a massive set of destructive earthquakes early in 2018 has triggered fears about the environment and the effects of large-scale mining operations on the land. Proper rituals to appease the earth would seem to be in order here as a global form of "repairing the land."

We have also shown how, in parts of the Highlands of Papua New Guinea, the elementary model of sacred revenge was at least partially transcended by competition among groups over the exchanges of wealth. Since sacred revenge lies at the heart of many forms of transgressive violent action in the world today, how could these processes be transmuted into gifts of positive exchange? If Papua New Guinea Highlanders were able to take a transformative leap of this kind, can the leaders of nation-states and unions of such states emulate such an evolution? Our discussion here ends on the brink of another realm of discussion, comparable to the mindful and ethical concerns of Marcel Mauss in the conclusion of his seminal work *The Gift* (Mauss 1969).

References

Douglas, Mary. 1966. *Purity and Danger: An Analysis of Concepts of Pollution and Taboo*. London: Routledge and Kegan Paul.

Homer. 1996. *The Odyssey*. Translated by Robert Fagles, with notes and Introduction by Bernard Knox. London and New York: Penguin Books.

Keesing, Roger M. 1992. *Custom and Confrontation: The Kwaio Struggle for Cultural Autonomy*. Chicago: University of Chicago Press.

Kelly, Raymond. 2000. *Warless Societies and the Origin of War*. Ann Arbor: University of Michigan Press.

Knauft, Bruce. 1985. *Good Company and Violence: Sorcery and Social action in a Lowland New Guinea society*. Berkeley: University of California Press.

Kuschel, Rolf. 1998. *Vengeance Is Their Reply: Blood Feud and Homicide in Bellona Island*. Copenhagen: Dansk Psykologisk Forlag (2 vols.)

  1999. "Aspects of Social Stratification and Honor on Pre-Christian and Modern Mungki (Bellona), with Angikinui F. Takiika and Kiu Angiki." *South Pacific Journal of Psychology* 11.1: 54–70.

Mauss, Marcel. 1969. *The Gift. Forms and Functions of Exchange in Archaic Societies*. Translated by Ian Cunnison. London: Cohen and West. (French original published in 1925.)

Monberg, Torben. 1991. *Bellona Island: Beliefs and Rituals*. Honolulu: University of Hawai'i Press.

Rappaport, Roy. 1968. *Pigs for the Ancestors: Ritual in the Ecology of a New Guinea People*. New Haven, CT: Yale University Press.

Riebe, Inge. 1991. "Do We Believe in Witchcraft?" In Andrew Pawley, ed., *Man and a Half: Essays in Pacific Anthropology and Ethnobiology in Honour of Ralph Bulmer*, pp. 317–326. Memoir No. 48. Auckland, New Zealand: Polynesian Society.

References

Stewart, Pamela J., and Andrew Strathern. 2002a. *Remaking the World: Myth, Mining and Ritual Change among the Duna of Papua New Guinea.* Smithsonian Series in Ethnographic Inquiry. Washington, DC: Smithsonian Institution Press.

2002b. *Gender, Song, and Sensibility: Folktales and Folksongs in the Highlands of New Guinea.* Westport, CT and London: Praeger Publishers (Greenwood Publishing).

2002c. *Humors and Substances: Ideas of the Body in New Guinea.* Westport, CT: Praeger Publishing.

2002d. *Violence: Theory and Ethnography.* London and New York: Continuum Publishing.

2004. *Witchcraft, Sorcery, Rumors and Gossip.* Cambridge: Cambridge University Press.

2008. *Exchange and Sacrifice.* Ritual Studies Monograph Series. Durham, NC: Carolina Academic Press.

Stewart, Pamela J., Andrew Strathern, and Juergen Trantow. 2011. *Melpa-German-English Dictionary.* Pittsburgh: University of Pittsburgh Library System.

Strathern, A. J. 1971 (Re-issued and updated, 2007). *The Rope of Moka.* Cambridge: Cambridge University Press.

1979. *Ongka: A Self-Account by a New Guinea Big-Man.* New York: St. Martin's Press.

Strathern, A. J. and Pamela J. Stewart. 1999a. "Outside and Inside Meanings: Non-Verbal and Verbal Modalities of Agonistic Communication among the Wiru of Papua New Guinea." *Man and Culture in Oceania* Vol. 15. pp. 1–22.

1999b. The Spirit is Coming! A Photographic-Textual Exposition of the Female Spirit Cult Performance in Mt. Hagen. Ritual Studies Monograph Series, Monograph No. 1. Pittsburgh.

References

1999c. *Collaborations and Conflicts. A Leader Through Time*. Fort Worth, TX: Harcourt Brace College Publishers.

2000a. *Arrow Talk: Transaction, Transition, and Contradiction in New Guinea Highlands History*. Kent, OH, and London: Kent State University Press.

2000b. "Dangerous Woods and Perilous Pearl Shells: The Fabricated Politics of a Longhouse in Pangia, Papua New Guinea." *Journal of Material Culture* 5(1): 69–89.

2001. "Rappaport's Maring: The Challenge of Ethnology." In *Ecology and the Sacred: Engaging the Anthropology of Roy Rappaport*, Ellen Messner and Michael Lambek (eds.),pp. 277–290. Ann Arbor: University of Michigan Press.

2004a. "Cults, Closures, Collaborations." In *Women as Unseen Characters. Male Ritual in Papua New Guinea*. Social Anthropology in Oceania Monograph Series, edited by Pascale Bonnemere,pp. 120–138. Philadelphia, PA: University of Pennsylvania Press.

2004b. *Empowering the Past, Confronting the Future, The Duna People of Papua New Guinea*. Contemporary Anthropology of Religion Series, New York: Palgrave Macmillan.

2007. Preface to the New Edition. "Waves of Change," pp. xv–xviii. In *The Rope of Moka*. [Re-issued with corrections, 2007]. Cambridge: Cambridge University Press.

2010. *Second Edition, Curing and Healing: Medical Anthropology in Global Perspective* [Updated and Revised]. Durham, NC: Carolina Academic Press.

2011. *Peace-Making and the Imagination*. St. Lucia, Brisbane: University of Queensland Press.

2013. "Religion and Violence in Pacific Island Societies." In Mark Juergensmeyer, Margo Kitts, and Michael Jerryson eds. *The Oxford*

References

Handbook of Religion and Violence, pp. 167–182. New York: Oxford University Press.

Trompf, G. W. 1991. *Payback. The Logic of Retribution in Melanesian Religion.* Cambridge: Cambridge University Press.

Wagner, Roy. 1981. *Habu: The Innovation of Meaning in Daribi Religion.* Chicago: University of Chicago Press

Wiessner, Polly and Akii Tumu. 1998. *Historical Vines: Enga Networks of Exchange, Ritual, and Warfare in Papua New Guinea.* Bathurst, N.S.W., Australia: Crawford House Publishing.

Wright, S. Fowler. 1946. *The Witchfinder.* London: Books of Today.

Acknowledgments

We would like to thank the staff members at Cambridge University Press who have assisted us in the production of this Element. We thank our series editors, Prof. Margo Kitts and Prof. James Lewis, for their support for our project, and especially Margo for helpful conversations about this topic via email and in Hawai'i. We also wish to thank the many people that we have worked with in our global traverses, stays, and movements. In particular, we express our thanks to all the people who have collaborated with us in the field and at institutions where we have been based while conducting research and lecturing. Sections of this manuscript were composed while staying in Bavaria where we were serving as guest professors at the University of Augsburg, Germany, in 2018, teaching a masters course, Medical Anthropology: Alternative Healing Practices and Ecology. We want to thank all of our kind sponsors and helpers in Augsburg over the years, especially Professor Klaus-Dieter Post (now, sadly, passed away), Professor Guenther Kronenbitter, Dr. Ina Hagen-Jeske, Dr. Carolin Ruther, and Julia Eberl of the Department of European Ethnology. Assistance from the Center for European Studies, University Center for International Studies, at the University of Pittsburgh, and its Director, Professor Jae-Jae Spoon, and Associate Director, Dr. Allyson Delnore, is also gratefully acknowledged.

Finally, very sincere thanks to the anonymous reviewer of this Element, who gave it much careful thought and made many fruitful suggestions for the expansion and clarification of its arguments. Considerations of space have meant that not all of those thoughts can be included here, but they will accompany us on further scholarly journeys in the stream of our activities.

Cambridge Elements

Religion and Violence

James R. Lewis
University of Tromsø

James R. Lewis is Professor of Religious Studies at the University of Tromsø, Norway, and the author and editor of a number of volumes, including *The Cambridge Companion to Religion and Terrorism*.

Margo Kitts
Hawai'i Pacific University

Margo Kitts edits the *Journal of Religion and Violence* and is Professor and Coordinator of Religious Studies and East-West Classical Studies at Hawai'i Pacific University in Honolulu.

ABOUT THE SERIES

Violence motivated by religious beliefs has become all too common in the years since the 9/11 attacks. Not surprisingly, interest in the topic of religion and violence has grown substantially since then. This Elements series on Religion and Violence addresses this new, frontier topic in a series of approximately fifty individual Elements. Collectively, the volumes will examine a range of topics, including violence in major world religious traditions, theories of religion and violence, holy war, witch hunting, and human sacrifice, among others.

ISSNs: 2397-9496 (online), 2514-3786 (print)

Cambridge Elements

Religion and Violence

ELEMENTS IN THE SERIES

A full series listing is available at: www.cambridge.org/ERAV

Printed in the United States
By Bookmasters